OTHER BOOKS BY RICHARD CURTIS

THE CASE FOR EXTINCTION

(with Professor Morton Stultifer, Hon. Ph.D.)

NOT EXACTLY A CRIME

OUR VICE PRESIDENTS FROM ADAMS TO AGNEW

by Richard Curtis and Maggie Wells

The Dial Press · *New York, 1972*

Grateful acknowledgment is made to the following for permission to reproduce the illustrations that appear on the following pages:

Page 45: From *Iron and Brass Implements of English and American Houses* by John Seymour. Courtesy Alec Tiranti Limited.

Page 82: From *This Was Burlesque.* Copyright © 1968 by Ann Corio and Joseph Dimona. Published by Grosset & Dunlap, Inc. Courtesy the publisher and Mr. Woodrow Gelman.

Page 86: Courtesy City of Manchester Art Galleries.

Page 103: From *American Science and Invention* by Mitchell Wilson. Courtesy Simon & Schuster, Inc.

Page 109: Courtesy The American Museum of Natural History.

Page 182: Courtesy Wide World Photos, Inc.

Page 187: Courtesy Schwenkfelder Library.

Library of Congress Cataloging in Publication Data

Curtis, Richard.
    Not exactly a crime.

      I. Vice-Presidents—U. S.—Anecdotes, facetiae, satire, etc. I. Wells, Maggie, joint author.
II. Title.
E176.C93   353'.0318'0207   79-37466

To the memories of Ken Stone, a poet and a prince, and Charles M. Wells, who always hoped for the best

Th' Prisidincy is th' highest office in th' gift iv th' people. Th' Vice-Prisidincy is th' next highest an' th' lowest. It isn't a crime exactly. Ye can't be sint to jail f'r it, but it's a kind iv a disgrace. It's like writin' anonymous letters.

MR. DOOLEY (FINLEY PETER DUNNE)

Contents

The names of the vice presidents have been
changed to spare their loved ones further grief.

· 1 ·

"In This, I am Nothing."

JOHN ADAMS

vice president under George Washington, 1789–1797

You'd think, being the first vice president, John Adams might have earned himself a catchy nickname like Uncle of His Country. Stepfather? But he didn't, and the fault is largely his for not making the best of a bad situation.

Right off the bat, Adams started bad-mouthing his new job. The first thing he said after being elected vice president was, "I am the vice president." Then, realizing this was not as auspicious as it could be, he added, "In this, I am nothing." Neither remark is the kind that gets you carved on Mount Rushmore, but Adams's lack of enthusiasm is understandable.

In the first place, he'd had better jobs—as a country lawyer in Massachusetts, for instance. Secondly, he won the vice presidency in what he himself called a "scurvey manner," thanks to the intrigues of Alexander

Hamilton, a fellow Federalist (which is what they called Republicans in those days). Hamilton finally intrigued himself into a fatal duel with another vice president, but that comes later.

When this country first started having elections, the winner got to be president and the runner-up, vice president. In the 1789 election, John Adams limped into second place with less than half the electoral vote. It was worse than losing because it was so noticeable.

When he heard the results, he was so embarrassed he refused to be vice president. He finally accepted, but only after convincing himself that the country would come apart at the seams if he didn't.[1]

Adams was closer to the mark when he reviewed his duties and declared, "My country has in its wisdom contrived for me the most insignificant office that ever the invention of man contrived or his imagination conceived." With that attitude, how could he be expected to give it the old college try?

There probably wouldn't have been a vice presidency, or a presidency for that matter, if it weren't for his zealot of a cousin, Sam. Samuel Adams was a patriot, which in those days was the term applied to someone who refused to Buy British. Revolutionizing in Boston was uphill work. Beacon Hill was the center of Anglophilia[2] in the colonies, and Sam put in a lot of overtime to get the American Revolution rolling.

Sam's job wasn't made any easier by some of the things Cousin John did, such as defending the British troops who took part in the Boston Massacre. The way the British told it, this surly crowd gathered in front of the British barracks in Boston and started hurling snowballs and oys-

---

1. It didn't until a few weeks ago.
2. And still is.

ter shells at nine British soldiers. One soldier, holding his musket in front of his face to fend off the missiles, slipped,[3] and his gun flew out of his hand and discharged into the crowd. Believing they were being sniped at, the other eight fired too, killing five demonstrators. Sound familiar?

As legal counsel to the soldiers was not a popular position, John Adams was bitterly reviled by his countrymen, and how he got elected to the Massachusetts House of Representatives the very next year by a vote of 418 to 118 is a mystery. But Adams examined the facts of the massacre in the cool light of reason—and this was *the* Age of Reason, remember —and concluded the soldiers were right. Besides, no one else would take the case. The commanding officer and all but two soldiers were acquitted; the two were branded on the hand and told to be more careful about massacring people in the future.

Not all of Adams's clients were unpopular, though. On another occasion he helped John Hancock, the famous handwriter, beat a smuggling rap brought against him by the British.[4]

As the Revolution began to shape up, Adams went to Philadelphia to join the Continental Congress and become a Founding Father. According to one historian, his chief contribution to the breach with England was to second Richard Henry Lee's famous resolution in the Congress that "these colonies are, and of a right ought to be, free and independent states."[5]

---

3. Yeah, sure.

4. Adams shrewdly resorted to the well-known legal gambit, *Omnem crede diem tibi diluxisse supremum. Grata superveniet quae non sperabitur hora. Me pinguem et nitidum bene curata cute vises cum ridere voles Epicuri de grege porcum.*

5. When historians start making a big deal about seconding something, you just know they don't have that much good material.

At length the Revolution began, though most colonists were skeptical at first. In those edgy times patriots were always jumping on their horses and galloping from town to town saying the British were coming, the British were coming, but the British never showed up. Posterity has enshrined Paul Revere only because at the particular time he rode out into the countryside the British *were* coming.

Adams was on the committee assigned to write the Declaration of Independence, but they decided to leave the job to Thomas Jefferson because he had a better way with words. But Adams did defend the Declaration in debate, at least, and despite his quirky predilection for defending British soldiers he was placed at the head of the board of war.

After the war,[6] Adams was appointed this nation's first minister to the Court of St. James's.[7] There everybody snubbed his wife, Abigail, in spite of the fact that she was a Quincy. The Quincys were a socially prominent Boston family whose name meant more then than it does now, except in England where it has never meant anything at any time. Adams's marriage to a Quincy turned him into a snob (he was also fat and got fatter as he went along), and his snobbishness may have cost him election to the first presidency of the United States. It seems that in a work he wrote defending the Constitution[8] he had suggested that "the rich, the well-born and the able" should be set apart from other men in a senate. This rubbed thirty-five out of sixty-nine electors the wrong way, and they cast their votes for George Washington.

---

6. Which we won. It was in all the papers.
7. St. James was the king of England then.
8. Turgot had attacked it. He said it was no good.

As he had defended the Constitution, he knew that the only thing a vice president had to do was preside over the Senate and wait for tie votes. The longer he was in office, the more he wished he hadn't defended that part of the Constitution. It didn't allow him to talk in the Senate unless there was a tie, but he talked anyway, joining in on debates and lecturing senators when they got out of hand. This continued until the Pennsylvania Congressional Delegation complained. From then on he confined his activities to presiding and tie-breaking. He holds the record —twenty-nine—for the number of tie-breaking votes cast by a vice president.

Finding himself with a lot of spare time, Adams began to worry about the wrong things. One of the first was how George Washington and other dignitaries (including himself) should be addressed. He pondered such titles for Washington as Your Majesty, Your Excellency, and Your Highness. When the question of how Adams should be addressed was presented to the Senate, someone suggested he be called His Rotundity. Benjamin Franklin wanted to call him Your Superfluous Excellency.

As noted earlier, Adams wasn't much of a vote getter, but he did manage to beat Thomas Jefferson by three electoral votes in the 1797 presidential election. Jefferson, a Republican (which is what they called Democrats in those days) and therefore a political enemy of Adams, then became vice president. Needless to say, the two differed on everything ranging from the Basic Goodness of Man (which Adams didn't buy) to which side to root for in the European wars following the French Revolution. Adams backed the English and started an undeclared war against France. It was not to be our last undeclared war. There was also the XYZ Affair around this time, but it's too complicated to explain.

John Adams was tactless, sharp-tongued, bad-tempered, and suspicious, and these qualities cost him a second term as president and all hope of being called Your Majesty—though there are those who insist his defeat was due to Abigail's habit of hanging her wash in the East Room of the brand-new White House. The thing is, all that rooting for the French in the next office got on Adams's nerves, so he retaliated with the Alien and Sedition acts enabling the government to deport or punish people who knocked his policies. The Alien Act was never invoked, but the Sedition Act was: one of the ten convictions obtained under it was meted out to someone who said that President Adams was filled with "ridiculous pomp, foolish adulation, and a selfish avarice." Some people just have thin skin.

Thomas Jefferson called the acts unconstitutional and said that if Adams had his way he'd make the country into the very kind we had just rebelled against. Adams could no longer see what was wrong with that. But everyone else could and he lost the election. Adams was so mad, he refused to go to Jefferson's inauguration, which shows what a poor sport he was on top of everything else.

It's silly to imagine that Abigail Adams's habit of hanging her wash in the East Room cost Adams a second term as president. When guests were expected, she took it down, or sometimes, if it was still damp, hid it behind a cluster of potted palms.

· 2 ·

"Honorable and Easy"

THOMAS JEFFERSON
vice president under John Adams, 1797–1801

Thomas Jefferson was a health nut and tinkerer who is best remembered as the inventor of the swivel chair, which in turn made possible the advent of modern bureaucracy.

In Jefferson's day, most people of any account were born rich and died richer. The log cabin rage didn't start till much later. Jefferson, however, gave trends a setback by being born rich and dying broke. He would have ended up all right if he'd stuck to inventing, but his weakness was dabbling.

He became a rich orphan at fourteen when his planter father died, leaving Thomas a house named Shadwell, 2750 acres of land, and a complete set of slaves. The boy was not satisfied, however; he longed for an education. So he bid farewell to Shadwell and his slaves and set out for the big city, as Williamsburg, Virginia, was thought of then.

While studying at William and Mary College, Jefferson became a fierce advocate of religious freedom. The reason is, the church of England enjoyed a spiritual monopoly in Williamsburg and could put people to death for missing three Sunday services. Also, if you got caught swearing twice, they could bore a hole through your tongue with an awl. Small wonder the church was packed every Sunday and even Patrick Henry, who drank a lot and was always sounding off at the local tavern, confined his speech to political slogans and other harmless rhetoric.

Jefferson didn't gamble or play cards, but he spent more time at taverns than most scholars like to admit. His vice, if any, was music. He adored playing his fiddle and took it along to parties, where he scraped away at hit tunes at the drop of a hat.[9] He was also into dancing in spite of big feet. He said it was good exercise, and Thomas Jefferson was absolutely bonkers on the subject of exercise. He loved to ride but pooh-poohed it as exercise because the horse did most of the work. He also took daily two-hour walks carrying an Early American firing piece, which weighed a ton.

After finishing his studies, he hung around Williamsburg practicing law and serving in the House of Burgesses (which is what they called the state house of representatives). Then in 1770 his absentee landlordship caught up with him: Shadwell burned to the ground. This forced him to build a new house, which he called Monticello.[10] He installed many of his own inventions, including a double door, either of whose halves opened when you pushed the other half.[11] This device is still used today, in Monticello at any rate.

---

9. Most of the hats dropped had three corners.
10. Because it was the first name that came to mind.
11. Here's a hint: it's done with secret chains shaped like figure eights.

After finishing Monticello with its double door, either of whose halves opened when you pushed the other half, Jefferson got married to a woman too feeble to bear him more than six children. Then she died, leaving him with little to do but serve his country. He hadn't done badly up to then, what with drafting the Declaration of Independence, membership in the Virginia House of Burgesses, and the governorship of Virginia (after Patrick Henry, whose political slogans had finally caught on with the voters).

In 1784 Jefferson was sent to France to replace Benjamin Franklin, who was tired. Franklin had originally been sent to negotiate trade agreements, but he spent as much time dallying with duchesses as he did promoting American salt cod and fish oil. That's why he was so darned tired. Thomas Jefferson, on the other hand, was strictly salt cod and fish oil. But though he didn't dally, he dabbled like a mad thing.

He wrote the first American tourist guide, advising travelers to explore the ramparts of a foreign city first to get an idea of the lay of the land. Ramparts lacking, try steeples. If there are no ramparts and no steeples, you should ask yourself what compelled you to visit the city in the first place. He also thought tourists should mainly confine their observations to agriculture and architecture. As for manufacturing methods, it was not likely that the United States would soon become a manufacturing country.[12] He also dismissed statues and paintings as "worth seeing, but not studying" and too expensive for Americans.[13]

---

12. Ha ha ha. He sure blundered there.

13. He had a point there. If you're going to start a country, you really ought to concentrate on food and shelter.

Unlike Benjamin Franklin, Jefferson felt uneasy with French women because they "wrinkled their foreheads with politics." His distaste focused on Marie Antoinette, about whom he wrote home, "Something should certainly be done about the wretched, dissipated, slippery, half-witted little queen."[14]

Such was Thomas Jefferson's reputation for honesty that few men ever questioned his veracity. One was Count Georges de Buffon, a famous French naturalist who cornered Jefferson at a soiree with the theory that hot countries produced large animals and moist countries, small ones. Jefferson asked what about the North American moose? Buffon denied there was any such animal. So Jefferson wrote a friend in New Hampshire asking him to kill a moose and send it to him in Paris. In due time it arrived. Buffon conceded there was such a thing as a moose.[15]

Jefferson, quite the opposite of testy old John Adams, was a good sport about becoming vice president. Jefferson pretended it was just what he wanted—that it was "honorable and easy" and would leave him lots of spare time for tinkering and investigating. Which it did. He invented a hemp beater, which was used to beat hemp. He also won a French prize for his design of a streamlined plow, and a leather buggy top he devised is still in use in spite of diminished demand. He also invented the dollar, the dime, and the penny, as well as the ten-dollar gold piece and the silver dollar.

---

14. Something finally was. Jefferson, incidentally, was all for the French Revolution and even offered his services as a consultant, since the French had never conducted a revolution before.

15. He then asked Jefferson to please throw it away as it had been in the warm hold of a ship for quite some time.

This is Jefferson's friend in New Hampshire who sent a dead moose to Paris when Jefferson asked him to. He had an awful time packing the antlers.

Some of his ideas were better than others. He once sketched out a plan for admitting new states, with proposed names such as Pelipsia, Cherronesus, Metropotamia, and Polypotamia to the Union.[16] He also had an idea for an easy way to build a Panama Canal: if you dug even a small trench across the isthmus, the Gulf Stream would rush in, widening and deepening it until it was navigable.

Jefferson was a lousy farmer and ran Monticello into the ground, but he nevertheless maintained a lively interest in agriculture throughout his life. Looking back on his life's achievements, he measured his importation of olive trees from France and rice from Africa as more important than his signing of the Declaration of Independence.[17] He was always sending rice home from somewhere and once smuggled a sack of it out of Turin.

In 1801 it was Jefferson's turn to be president. In his first inaugural speech he said, "We are all Republicans, we are all Federalists." A lot of people thought they knew what he meant but weren't completely sure.

All his life Thomas Jefferson was for the consent of the governed and that sort of thing. John Adams, a dedicated Federalist, felt just the opposite. On July 4, 1826, the Golden Anniversary of the signing of the Declaration of Independence, Adams breathed his last. Not to be outdone, Jefferson followed suit four hours later. That's carrying a feud pretty far.

---

16. Only one of these, Pelipsia, joined.
17. To each his own.

· 3 ·

"Embryo Caesar"

AARON BURR
vice president under Thomas Jefferson, 1801–1805

A hypochondriac with a weakness for widows, a penchant for dueling, and a passion for plotting, Aaron Burr was all the bad things a minister's son is supposed to be. He is the only United States vice president to preside over the Senate while under indictment for murder; and as ex-vice president, he managed to get himself tried for treason. In short, a very heavy dude.

His early life was conventional enough. His father died shortly after founding Princeton University, and his mother presently followed after observing that little Aaron was "sly and mischievous." At ten the youth tried to run away to sea. Unhappily for Alexander Hamilton and a lot of other people, somebody stopped him.

He entered Princeton at the age of thirteen, having been turned down two years earlier because of his size.[18] Nobody ever said Aaron Burr wasn't smart. He breezed through Princeton, sticking to his books and ignoring the religious fervors that periodically swept American campuses before the advent of football. After graduation, Burr toyed with the idea of becoming a minister, which was good steady work in those days. But his fun-loving nature rejected it, and he set out instead to be a lawyer, though what fun there is in that it's hard to say. Meanwhile, the American Revolution had begun, and Burr didn't want to miss it.

With Benedict Arnold, whose name was not yet mud, Burr set out for Quebec, whence he returned a hero. It didn't take much. He disguised himself as a French priest and took a note to General Richard Montgomery. Then, when Montgomery was shot during the attack on Quebec, Burr dragged his body a few feet from where it fell. Since Montgomery was already dead, it's not easy to see what difference this made.

Nevertheless, he was rewarded with an appointment to George Washington's staff. Unfortunately, Burr and Washington failed to hit it off. Burr, who was twenty years old[19] and something of a swinger, considered Washington stiff and humorless. There was some truth to this, as Washington's teeth caused him a great deal of discomfort. Washington disliked Burr for a better reason: he caught him reading his mail.

To put things right, John Hancock arranged for Burr to be transferred to the staff of a more amiable general named Israel Putnam. They got along just fine. Their military exploits included an expedition to rout

---

18. He was fourteen inches high.
19. He had grown to normal stature by then.

the British from Flatbush, not far from the future site of Ebbets Field.

Burr also took part in the Battle of Monmouth. He was so worn out after the battle, he lay down under a tree and fell asleep, and when he woke up he was suffering from sunstroke.

Burr was dogged by ill health all his life, though he would always leap out of his sickbed to fight the British. His favorite headache remedy was to sit drinking camomile tea, with his feet soaking in warm water and his head wrapped in a vinegar-soaked cloth. Or was it feet in camomile tea, head wrapped in warm water-soaked cloth, drinking vinegar? Anyway, it worked: Burr lived to be eighty.

Alienating Washington and catching sunstroke did not deter Burr from being a good soldier. He detested looting and other "uncivilized" aspects of warfare, and reform was the keynote of his commands. His attention to detail was awesome. At one point, he ordered his soldiers to search the stays of the local camp followers in case they might be smuggling secrets to the British in their corsets.

It's a wonder Burr didn't search them himself. Abstemious in everything else and uninterested in gambling, his one vice was women. And widow ladies had a particularly stimulating effect on him. He liked widows so much he sometimes didn't even wait until they were widows.

Searching the stays of camp followers was more fun than, say, KP, and many militiamen actually volunteered for this detail. This is a camp follower whose stays have just been searched. The letters refer to corners of her stays in which Burr suspected she might tuck a message for the British.

He met his first wife, Theodosia, in Newark, New Jersey, while the war was still going on and she was married to a British officer named Provost who was conveniently stationed in Jamaica. Surrounded by the American Revolution, Theodosia offered the hospitality of her house to the Americans, among them Aaron Burr. They became pen pals.

Meanwhile, Burr was meeting with Washington, doing a little spying, and generally keeping his hand in things until his constitution, weakened by that sunstroke, forced him to resign from the army. Back in Albany, struggling to establish himself as a lawyer, Burr kept on writing to Mrs. Provost, whose husband had obliged by dying in Jamaica. Eventually, Aaron and Theodosia got married and moved into a house on Wall Street in New York.

Burr began to prosper as a lawyer. He seldom, if ever, lost a case, so politics was a logical next step. He got himself elected to the New York state legislature in 1784. Meanwhile, he had fallen into a rivalry with another sharp lawyer, Alexander Hamilton. Hamilton was a Federalist, Burr ostensibly a Whig.

We say "ostensibly" because unless one was a Federalist, it was difficult to be sure what one was in those days. Thomas Jefferson, who was dead set against Federalism, was the leader of the opposition, who were sometimes called Anti-Federalists, at other times Jeffersonian Democrats, and at still others, Democratic-Republicans. In the South, these men were called Republicans; in the North, Democrats. And some people, like Aaron Burr, still used the word Whig, meaning you were against whoever was in office and kept your options open. Technically a Republican (or Whig, Anti-Federalist, or Democrat), Burr had many Federalist friends (except for Alexander Hamilton) and sometimes he agreed with their views. In fact, late in life he admitted he thought Jefferson (a Jeffersonian Democrat if there ever was one) a plain farmer with dangerous egalitarian ideas.[20]

Clearly, anyone with such built-in flexibility was predestined for political success. From the legislature, Burr proceeded to the United States Senate, beating Alexander Hamilton's father-in-law in the 1791 election and becoming the junior senator from New York, which took him to Philadelphia a lot.

In the meantime, Theodosia died. She had been ill for some time, though not from sunstroke. The best doctor in Philadelphia, Dr. Benjamin Rush, prescribed hemlock for whatever was ailing her. So at thirty Burr was left a widower with an eleven-year-old daughter who was also called Theodosia.

Though he remained a widower for four decades after his wife's death, nobody ever suspected him of celibacy during this period. An early romance with a Philadelphia socialite named Rebecca Smith, who had since married a man named Samuel Blodgett, Jr., revived in the spring of 1814 when Blodgett died[21] and Burr became executor of his estate, including Rebecca. Another friendly widow named Dorothea Todd named Burr sole guardian of her infant son when she became a widow in 1793. Burr fixed her up with James Madison, and the following year she became Dolly Madison.

---

20. Some of this is boring, but please pay attention. It gets better.
21. Husbands had a strange way of dying whenever Burr became interested in their wives. See? It *is* getting better!

Even without full support from either side, Burr managed to make a name for himself as a political innovator.[22] He all but invented the political machine, with himself at the center of a body of supporters called Burrites; he introduced music to political campaigning; was the first to recognize the vote-getting value of war heroes; and saw the value of befriending minorities. On the eve of one election, he gave a ball and supper at his house for "twenty gentlemen of colour." Another time he brought an Indian home for dinner, which was a pretty radical thing to do even though the Indian in question was the famous Captain Joseph Brant, king of the Mohawks. After a while, one presumes, Burr's cook got used to her employer sticking his head in the kitchen door and saying, "Guess who's coming to dinner?"

The problem was, nobody trusted Burr. Washington and Jefferson didn't like him, and neither did Alexander Hamilton. The wonder of it is that he almost became president.

In 1801 he and Jefferson tied for the presidency, which caused a great flap. The matter was referred to the House of Representatives, which took a week and thirty-six ballots to decide that Jefferson should be president and Burr, vice president. A good reason for the shift of votes is that Alexander Hamilton went around calling Burr an "embryo Caesar" and other not nice things.

Burr and Jefferson didn't get along any too well. The President never told Burr anything, so Burr got even by voting against Jefferson's ideas when they came to a tie vote in the Senate. Burr decided he wanted some

22. "Hustler" was the name.

other office and announced his candidacy for the New York governorship.

As soon as he heard the news, Alexander Hamilton rushed to New York and started meddling again, and Burr lost the election. As if that weren't bad enough, Hamilton said some really awful things about Burr,[23] most of which got into the newspapers. So Burr challenged Hamilton to a duel.

It was no match. Burr had lots more experience with duels than Hamilton; not that Burr had fought many duels, but he'd been around a lot. He'd even saved Hamilton from entering a duel with James Monroe in 1797. Also, a friend of Burr's had had a duel on his behalf with DeWitt Clinton.[24] Burr's only previous duel was with Hamilton's brother-in-law, John Church, who shot Burr through the coat.

Amid the ruins of his political career, Burr consoled himself with a lady from Philadelphia named Celeste while he waited for Hamilton to reply to his letter of the 18th inst. requesting an explanation of his insinuations. Hamilton didn't really want to duel, but he didn't want to explain either, so a date was set for July 11. A week before the big day both rivals attended the annual Fourth of July dinner given by the Society of Cincinnati at Fraunces Tavern. Burr looked glum, but Hamilton put on a good smile and sang a song called "The Drum."[25]

---

23. Like, "Burr's grandpa was a Puritan." Only, Burr's grandpa *was.* Burr's grandpa was Jonathan Edwards.
24. When it came to duels, Burr was a name-dropper.
25. Nobody we've asked knows how it goes.

To pass the time Burr wrote a will, leaving his best slave to his baby grandson and instructing his daughter to burn all his old love letters. On the morning of the eleventh, everybody rowed over to Weehawken, which was the In Place for Dueling in those days. Burr shot Hamilton and went home for breakfast.

Promptly upon dying, Hamilton became a hero. Everybody was so mad at Burr he had to lam out of New York and make his way to Philadelphia by way of Perth Amboy, New Jersey. In Philadelphia he was sheltered by a Biddle who didn't like Alexander Hamilton either (though he wouldn't have gone so far as to shoot him), and from there Burr fled to the South, where duels were more modish.

Burr headed for Florida, where everybody assumed he was on a spying mission. No one ever believed that Aaron Burr would do something just for the fun of it. But apparently, he just went there to look around.

While still under indictment for murder in New York and New Jersey, he returned to Washington to resume his vice presidential duties. His last act in office was to preside over the Senate trial of Supreme Court Justice Samuel Chase, who'd been haranguing juries on the evils of democracy and the danger of giving the vote to the common man. Burr handled the affair so fairly, even his enemies admired him. Chase was found innocent. Then Burr made such an eloquent farewell speech it caused one senator to weep for fifteen minutes.

Burr then set off for the West, hoping for a war with Spain. He hired an ark and sailed down the Ohio toward New Orleans. His first stop was Blennerhasset Island, where he stayed with Mr. and Mrs. Harman Blennerhasset, who were uncle and niece as well as man and wife.[26] Mrs. Blennerhasset's maiden name was Agnew.

Tearing himself away from the Blennerhassets, Burr drifted down the Ohio, pausing at Natchez and other cultural centers where dueling, spying, and plotting were more accepted than they were in Washington and New York. When he got to New Orleans, he went to work trying to get support for an empire that would consist of the newly purchased Louisiana Territory, a large portion of the American West, and all of Mexico. He was still trying to drum up sympathy for this grand scheme when he was arrested for treason in Mississippi in 1807.[27] When word of the arrest reached Washington, Thomas Jefferson confided in Congress that there was "no doubt" of his former vice president's guilt. Evidently the jury that heard the case thought differently, for Burr was acquitted.

Retired from active politics and plotting, Burr never quit dreaming. Long after his plan for a Western nation fizzled, he is rumored to have contacted Napoleon to discuss the feasibility of an attack on Boston. The exact purpose of this plan is not entirely clear.[28]

In his sunset years, Burr had a last, disastrous fling with a widow. She was one Mme. Elizabeth Jumel, and her past was checkered as the dickens. She bore an illegitimate child in her adolescence and abandoned him. Then a friendly sea captain took her to France,

---

26. There is nothing wrong with that and that is *not* why they lived on an island.
27. Don't *you* think he went too far?
28. Maybe he just didn't like Boston. It's a tough town if you don't know anybody.

where she acquired airs and a little polish.[29] Returning to New York, she became the mistress of a rich Frenchman named Stephen Jumel, who married her when she pretended to be fatally ill. Snubbed by New York society, the pair retreated to France, where everybody loved them. When they returned to try New York again, Jumel fell off a wagon and was killed.[30] Burr married the widow and plundered her fortune. A year later Mrs. Burr filed for divorce, charging him with infidelities with a number of women, including one Jane McManus of Jersey City.

29. Also a little Polish, from this millinery clerk from Cracow.
30. There! It happened again!

· 4 ·

"Old, Ill, Cranky and Ineffectual"

GEORGE CLINTON
vice president under Thomas Jefferson and
James Madison, 1805–April 30, 1812

George Clinton was picked for the vice presidency in 1804 because he had coped so effectively with the Indians in western New York. Folks figured that anyone who could handle Indians could handle senators.

What they didn't take into account was that by the time Clinton got to be vice president, he was so senile he'd forgotten how to count. Presiding over the Senate, where Lord only knows there's little enough to do, he kept miscounting votes, which caused a great deal of confusion.

He was far better at being governor of New York, but then he'd had more practice at it. He was governor of New York seven times, but vice president only twice.

The first time Clinton ever ran for the governorship, he scored a stunning upset victory over Philip Schuyler, who was one of *the* Schuylers.[31] Just to rub it in, Clinton won both the governorship *and* the lieutenant governorship. After thinking it over, he decided he'd rather have the governorship. This turned out to be the first of six consecutive terms, a longevity in office that approached a reign and earned him the title Father of His State, though no one thinks of him that way today.[32]

A good deal of Clinton's political success can be traced to the fact that he married Cornelia Tappan, who was related to the powerful Wynkoops. Oh come on, you've heard of the Wynkoops! The attraction was mutual. Clinton had been something of a war hero, having served as a brigadier general first in the militia and later in the Continental army.

Why Clinton bothered so about the American Revolution is a mystery, for he was opposed to the adoption of the Federal Constitution. He wasn't just lukewarm about it, mind you, he was against it. Oh, he had nothing against democracy, but basically he was more interested in New York than he was in the big picture. He believed that in time New York would become the financial center of the world and thought it should become a separate nation[33] with him as ruler.

Clinton was a top-notch prophet. In 1795 he had a feeling the Federalists were due to win an election, so he announced he would not seek a

31. Though, in all fairness, it must be pointed out that Clinton was one of *the* Clintons. De Witt was his nephew.
32. No one thinks of him at all today, in fact.
33. It finally did in 1934, but not too many people know about it.

seventh term. (He was one of those Anti-Federalist-Jeffersonian-Democratic-Whig-Republicans, you see.) As he had predicted, the Federalists won. But in 1800 Clinton made a comeback, announced he would seek a seventh term, and won.

Four years later Thomas Jefferson was up for another whack at the presidency, and Clinton was nominated for the vice presidency largely because the Democratic Republicans needed a Northerner to balance the ticket[34] and calm down all the wild talk about a Virginia Dynasty. Where that notion came from is hard to say: everybody seemed to forget that John Adams was from Massachusetts, and everyone else was dying to forget Aaron Burr, period.

As his dreams of a separate republic dwindled, Clinton decided to settle for second best. He tried for the vice presidency in 1788 and again in 1792. In 1800 it was that seventh New York governorship, then in 1804 another try for vice president. This time he made it, but by now he was "old, ill, cranky and ineffectual," though otherwise in top shape. He'd also forgotten how to count and made other mistakes that were hard to explain, like appointing duplicate committees. According to one account, he "whiled away much of his time at his boarding house."

John Quincy Adams, son of John Adams and a senator at the time, claimed that Clinton was "totally ignorant of the most common forms of proceeding" in the Senate. Clinton took this to mean the vice presidency

---

34. After the 1800 election resulting in Burr's tie with Jefferson, the Twelfth Amendment had been passed which called for separate votes for presidential and vice presidential candidates and eliminating the runner-up system. Some scholarly footnote, eh?

*When George Clinton
dropped dead at the age of
seventy-two the ship of state
sailed on smoothly without
him, or anybody else, for
that matter.*

wasn't good enough for him. When Jefferson's second term neared its end, Clinton made it known that he was ready to become president.

Now even his own party realized this was not a good idea. They picked James Madison instead and gave Clinton another turn at vice president as consolation. This time things were even worse. Clinton despised Madison and refused to attend the inauguration. He would not so much as say "Hello, Dolly" to the President's wife. Also, he sat around his boarding house telling everyone how stupid Madison's policies were.[35] It was a great relief to the nation when Clinton finally died in office at the age of seventy-two.

Fortunately, it was an election year, so the country wasn't without a vice president for long, and the ship of state sailed on relatively smoothly in the interim. About this time people began to suspect that the vice president was not all that important.

_____

35. Nephew De Witt, who must have sat in on some of these sessions, ran against Madison in 1812. Nephew De Witt lost.

· 5 ·

Hardly a Hero

ELBRIDGE GERRY
vice president under James Madison, 1813–1814

If Elbridge Gerry had had his way, there would have been no vice presidents at all. Back at the Constitutional Convention of 1787, after all the important considerations had been taken up, the delegates still had some time before lunch, so they discussed the possibility of working a vice president into the management chart.

Gerry fought the notion tooth and nail. He said right out that the office would be unnecessary. Nobody paid much attention because Gerry had also said the Constitution was "full of vices," which went against the grain of many delegates who'd been working hard to draw the thing up. Finally, Gerry declared that he wouldn't sign the Constitution if there was a vice president written into it. The delegates hooted and said, "Go ahead, see if we care." So Gerry distinguished himself by not signing the Constitution.[36]

In fact, if Gerry hadn't invented Gerrymandering (which we'll explain later), he'd hardly be worth mentioning. As soon as he graduated from Harvard, he went into the family business of shipping dried codfish to Barbados and Spanish ports. Then came the Revolution. While patriots were galloping all over the landscape, Gerry was hiding in a cornfield in his nightshirt.

The truth is, he was something of a snob, which made it hard for him to come out wholeheartedly in favor of the Revolution. During the warmup or "excited mob" phase, an excited mob burned down a smallpox hospital that Gerry and some of his friends had donated to the community. He was so upset he almost resigned from the Revolution.

During most of the war, Gerry was assigned a quartermastership because of his vast experience with dried codfish. Later, he was assigned to a committee in charge of establishing a United States navy, but nothing ever came of it.[37]

Elbridge Gerry was a prude as well as a snob. He tried to get Benjamin Franklin recalled from France because he said Franklin had been corrupted there. This was false. Franklin had been corrupted long before he got there. But Gerry was probably just jealous because *he* hadn't been corrupted. Gerry also went along with Sam Adams when Sam, for the

---

36. If you'll look very carefully at the lower left-hand corner of the Constitution, you won't find his name.
37. We have one now though.

*One of Elbridge Gerry's
revolutionary assignments
was to establish a United
States Navy. This is one
his early designs for an
American fleet, which
explains why nothing ever
came of it.*

sake of the Revolution prohibited the production of stage plays. It was the first time anything had ever been banned in Boston.

Gerry was one of those people who always think they're right and everybody else is wrong. At the Constitutional Convention, someone had remarked of Gerry that he "objected to everything he did not propose." No wonder he decided in 1793 to retire to his farm and educate his children.

In 1810, scouting around for a candidate, the Republicans invited him back to Boston to run for governor. They must have been really hard up. Gerry was no friend of the common man and disdained the democratic process. For instance, he never went to caucuses because he considered them "below his dignity." The common people of Boston hated him, but as luck would have it the opposition put up an even bigger snob named Christopher Gore, so Elbridge Gerry won the election.

While serving as governor, he pondered a way to outsmart the democratic system and make Massachusetts safe for Republicans. He finally hit on a plan for creating a legislative district that would encompass his home town of Marblehead—a hotbed of Republicanism—along with a lot of little Federalist towns in which he didn't live. This idea of creating legislative districts to suit one's political needs came to be known as Gerrymandering because the district Gerry invented was shaped like a salamander.[38]

Figuring that such deviousness should be rewarded, the Republicans nominated Gerry to run for the vice presidency along with James Madi-

---

38. More like a chameleon, actually, but Gerrychameleon sounds awkward.

son, then seeking a second term. All Madison wanted was a vice president who wore shoes and didn't despise him. Gerry was old and in frail health, and the Republicans assured Madison their boy wouldn't cause trouble. But Gerry didn't know when to keep his mouth shut.

Just as the War of 1812 was about to begin, Gerry grumbled that the United States had been too long at peace and if some sort of war didn't break out soon the country would degenerate into "a mere nation of traders."[39] He seemed to overlook the fact that if it hadn't been for the dried codfish trade, he would never have been able to afford a Harvard degree and probably would never have seen the inside of the statehouse. How quickly we forget!

Gerry reveled in the war, therefore, and so did Madison. But Madison's liver was frail, and three months after inauguration to his second term, it acted up and almost killed him. Everyone, including the French ambassador, was horrified at the prospect of a frail old snob like Gerry moving up to the presidency.[40]

But Madison recovered, and it was the frail old snob who collapsed in his coach and died less than two years after his election. This was the second vice president to die on Madison, and it made him feel rather spooky. A lot of people started to think that winning the vice presidency wasn't just a misfortune but a curse.

---

39. This was nonsense. It degenerated into a mere nation of traders and farmers.
40. This was highly improper for an ambassador to say. He should have kept his fat mouth shut.

· 6 ·

What Did You Do
With The $660,000?

DANIEL D. TOMPKINS
vice president under James Monroe, 1817–1825

The War of 1812 brought fame to some, disgrace to others. Dolly Madison became famous for giving lots of parties, keeping the President up late, and rescuing Gilbert Stuart's painting of George Washington when the British came to burn the White House down. Francis Scott Key became famous for writing a national anthem in the heat of battle. Andrew Jackson became famous for scoring the only American goal of the war.[41] Meanwhile, poor Daniel D. Tompkins got the job defending the state of New York but no funds to do it with.

---

41. But after the whistle had blown. Andrew Jackson won the Battle of New Orleans after the peace treaty was signed.

· 38 ·

He got the job because he'd been governor of New York and a good one at that. He improved the school system, liberalized the criminal code,[42] and reformed the militia. He was also in favor of the abolition of slavery and urged humane treatment of Negroes and Indians. Following a familiar path to political prosperity, he had married the daughter of a prominent Republican named Mangle Minthorne.

All these things (with the exception of his father-in-law's name) encouraged government leaders to select Tompkins as the perfect man to defend the New York frontier. A lesser fellow would have declined the honor on the basis that he could not afford it. But Tompkins pitched right in and did what he could.

It takes a lot of money to support twenty thousand soldiers, even militia men. So Tompkins borrowed money left and right. When his own credit was exhausted, he drew vast sums from the New York State treasury, to which he had access by virtue of the fact that he had served four terms as governor and thus was a familiar figure at the teller's window.

The job of commanding the New York militia kept Tompkins so busy he never had time to keep track of how much his war efforts were costing. When the war finally ended, Tompkins totted it all up as best he could and submitted an expense account of $660,000 to the United States government.

At this point, the entire accounting department of the United States of America fainted dead away from shock. While they were still coming to, Tompkins was nominated by the Republican party to run for the vice

---

42. For instance, before he took office the code for a felony was three dots and two dashes; after, two dots and a dash.

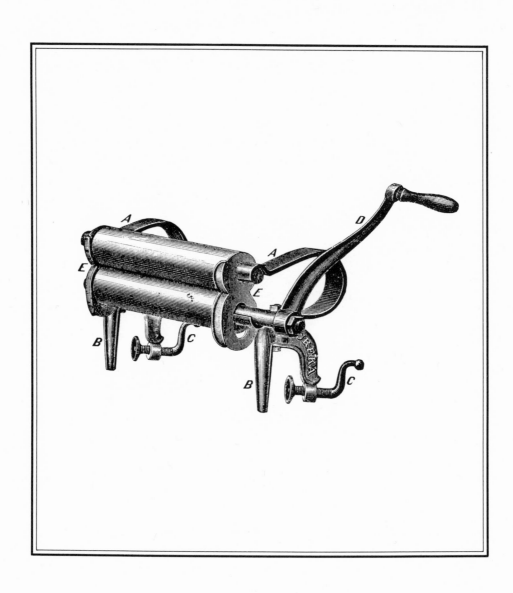

presidency. The reason he was picked was, the country was sick and tired of vice presidents dropping dead, and Tompkins was only forty-two years old.

It wasn't until after Tompkins was elected (his running mate, James Monroe, was elected president) that the accounting department recovered sufficiently to ask him to itemize that expense account. By that time, Tompkins no longer had any idea what he'd done with the $660,000. He'd just spent it defending the frontier of New York, that's all.

Well, you know accounting departments. An awful fuss ensued, and Tompkins was so hard pressed to remember where the money went he had little time left for tending the Senate. The government even withheld his pay until he could come up with an explanation.[43]

It was a real mess and never fully resolved. Poor Tompkins never did manage to clear his name, though the government finally paid him a paltry $95,000 for taking care of New York during the war. Nobody seemed to appreciate what he'd done. They just kept on harping about all that money. It was enough to get anybody down.

---

43. He earned $5000 a year. After 132 years in office the debt would be all paid back.

This attractive appliance, which was manufactured by the Eureka Clothes Wringing Machine Company in Waltham, Massachusetts, was called a mangle. Daniel Tompkins' father-in-law was also a Mangle.

·7·

A Southerner With a Gift of Gab

JOHN C. CALHOUN
*vice president under John Quincy Adams and
Andrew Jackson, 1825–December 28, 1832*

John C. Calhoun was a Southerner with a gift of gab who wanted to be vice president in the worst way. That's right, *vice* president. Maybe he just wanted to prove the office wasn't jinxed, which is what everybody was saying. Well, he didn't.

To accomplish his perverse ambition, he went to both major candidates, John Quincy Adams and Andrew Jackson, and promised his full support. Thus, when John Quincy Adams won the election of 1824, Calhoun's election as vice president went uncontested. Calhoun would have ended up as vice president even if Jackson had won. He presided over one of the classiest senates ever, with a whole pack of fine orators and no fewer than four future presidents.

It was hard for Calhoun, who was no mean talker himself, to sit there day after day just listening to the senators debate and not being able to pitch in and help. He spent a lot of this idle time trying to figure out whom to be nice to for the coming election of 1828. He came to the conclusion that Jackson was the man to watch and set out to convince the general that he was really his friend, appearances to the contrary. Jackson did turn out to be the man of the year in '28, but it was not Calhoun's scheming that gained him a second term as vice president.

Jackson's friends, who were trying to get Calhoun out of Andy's way, played a trick on Calhoun. They persuaded him to run for the vice presidency by convincing him that Jackson was fearfully ill and would probably not survive much beyond the inauguration. Calhoun's rosy vision of himself in the White House faded after election day when Jackson enjoyed a miraculous recovery from his mysterious ailment.[44]

Jackson was the first of the log cabin types that became so popular in the nineteenth century.[45] On the day of his inauguration, all the common people in the country crowded into Washington to celebrate. They stood on the chairs in the White House in their muddy boots, spit, and whacked each other on the back. They also drank a lot. It was a fearful experience for Calhoun, who had never seen a common person before.

Jackson had a secretary of war named Eaton, who along with Secretary of State Martin Van Buren was the only friend Jackson had in his own cabinet. The rest had been befriended by Calhoun, just in case any

44. Seventeen years later, when Jackson finally did die, Calhoun realized he'd been tricked.
45. Their popularity continued into the twentieth, as witness the election of Coolidge, Kennedy, and Nixon.

of them ever got to be president. The trouble was, Eaton had married a widow lady who'd been involved in a Personal Scandal. In that day and age a Personal Scandal could have meant anything. Some said she was messing around with Eaton before they got married. Maybe her hat fell off in church, or she had shaken hands with an Indian or something. Who can be sure?

The point is, nobody in Washington would have anything to do with Peggy Eaton, except Andrew Jackson and Martin Van Buren. Those were the days when ladies got all dressed up in the morning and paid calls on other ladies, then rushed home and sat in their own parlors waiting for the ladies they'd called on to call on them. Mrs. Eaton called on Mrs. Calhoun, then sat around her parlor for weeks waiting for Mrs. Calhoun to drop by. But Mrs. Calhoun didn't, nor did any other Washington ladies.

Andrew Jackson got so upset about this that he called for everyone in his cabinet to resign, including his friend Van Buren, so he could start all over from scratch. This was particularly vexing to Calhoun, because now he didn't know where to begin looking for someone who might become the next president.

Troubles always come in twos and threes, and Calhoun also found himself embroiled in arguments about slavery at this time. Being a Southerner, he didn't much cotton[46] to abolition. To counteract it, he came up with the Nullification Doctrine, which said that any state had the right to pronounce null and void any law it didn't like. Many Southerners preferred the idea of secession from the Union, but Calhoun ar-

---

46. This is a pun. "Cotton" means "to like," but it was also the crop that created slavery. There are twelve other puns in this book. Can you find them?

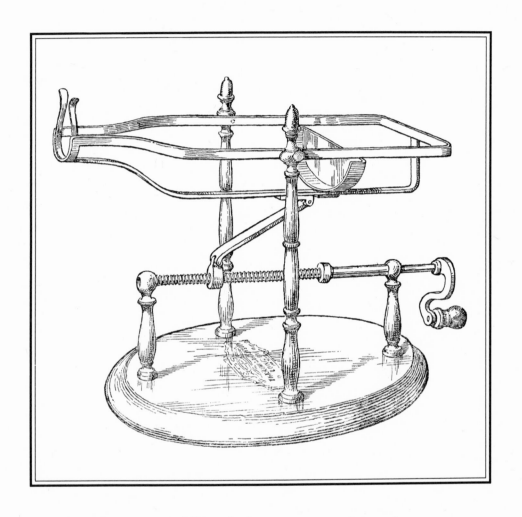

*Bottle tilter, possibly of the type used in the
1830 Jefferson Day Dinner toast, or possibly not.*

gued that Nullification was a five-syllable word. An awful lot of people were impressed. But when they thought about it, they realized it was just another way of saying Anarchy. After all, what if a town decided to nullify its state's nullification? And what if a citizen decided to nullify his town's nullification of the state's nullification? Sloppy thinking. Very sloppy thinking.

Though Jackson was a Southerner, no one was sure what he thought of Nullification. They found out at the Jefferson Day Dinner of 1830. He raised his glass and proposed a toast: "Our Union—it must be preserved!" Obviously, Jackson had picked up on Calhoun's sloppy thinking. Calhoun drank the toast, but he wasn't happy about it. Word soon went out that Calhoun would not be running for the vice presidency in the next election, no matter who ran for president.

This made his duties in the Senate hard to carry out. Friends of President Jackson kept insulting Calhoun indirectly in their speeches, and because of the Constitution he had to sit there and take it. If only there was some way to nullify some of those s.o.b.'s, he said to himself. Finally he got so fed up, he quit. He is the only vice president who did, though all of them wished they could, at one point or another. Back in the South, Calhoun was a hero. His home state of South Carolina sent him back to Washington as a senator, and he finally had a chance to debate with Daniel Webster and say all the things he'd been storing up to say as vice president.

· 8 ·

The Little Magician

MARTIN VAN BUREN
vice president under Andrew Jackson, 1833–1837

What, you might well ask, was a nice guy like Martin Van Buren doing in the vice presidency?

Unlike John C. Calhoun, who was nice to Andrew Jackson but perfectly horrid to Peggy Eaton, Van Buren was nice to both. He chatted with Mrs. Eaton at parties where nobody else would even get her a glass of punch. This earned him Andrew Jackson's deepest gratitude, because Andrew Jackson was completely teed off at all the snobs in Washington who had made him get rid of a perfectly good cabinet on Mrs. Eaton's account.

Temperamentally, Van Buren was ideally suited for politics. He was honest, which it was getting harder and harder to be in politics,[47] and he

---

47. Today it is easy, as long as you are rich.

was friendly, witty, cheerful, and resourceful. His cohorts called him The Little Magician, because he could accomplish with honesty things they couldn't accomplish with chicanery.

Undoubtedly, a happy childhood had something to do with it. The elder Van Burens were frugal truck farmers who kept a tavern, saved their money, and eventually became "respectable, slave-owning citizens." Little Martin grew up, but not much. At the peak of his career, he was barely five and a half feet tall[48]—a trim, dandified dresser with blond, curly hair that turned to rust color as it swept into sideburns, or Burnsides as they were called then.[49]

A staunch Republican, which you'll remember was the contemporary term for Democrat,[50] Van Buren had no trouble moving up from the New York State Assembly to the United States Senate. He befriended Andrew Jackson, who liked the kid's stuff and asked him to be his secretary of state.

Jackson depended on Van Buren for other things besides being nice to maligned widows. Van Buren helped Jackson write his famous anti-nullification toast—the one that upset Calhoun so. When you consider that the toast consisted of only six words, you can understand how badly Jackson needed help and how grateful he was to anyone who could provide it.

When he finally got rid of his cabinet, Andrew Jackson was deter-

---

48. After his peak, he lost about two inches a year.
49. Gotcha! Burnsides were named after General A. E. Burnside, who fought in the Civil War a generation later. Stay on your toes.
50. *Please* try to remember this!

*Sideburns can lend a touch of distinction
to an otherwise undistinctive appearance.
But it must also be noted that they can detract
from one's appearance and even impair one's
hearing if left to grow wild.*

mined to save Van Buren. Since no important toasts were coming up, he sent him off to England as United States minister. Jackson did this without waiting for Senate confirmation, which was good because if he'd waited, Van Buren would never have gotten to see Europe.

As it was, Van Buren went to England in August, 1831, and the English found him enchanting.[51] When the Senate reconvened and found out what had happened, it rejected Van Buren's appointment for no better reason than to satisfy John C. Calhoun. When the news reached Van Buren, he simply stopped ministering to the English and went for a trip through France and Holland with his son, John. He was still enjoying his travels on the continent when he was nominated for the vice presidency, which shows he had friends where it counts.

Van Buren's nomination to the vice presidency is interesting because it was the first to take place at a convention, earlier ones having been made at congressional caucuses. This was supposed to be a reform, but if you've ever been to a convention you'll agree that Van Buren was lucky to be in Europe.

He got a great welcome when he sailed back to New York and was elected with Jackson in 1832. He went on to perform his vice presidential duties in what one account calls a "routine, undistinguished fashion." Compared to most of his predecessors, that was a prodigious achievement.

By not talking out of turn or miscounting votes in the Senate, and by not committing any acts of treason or indulging in moral turpitude or

---

51. He could do card tricks and pull tablecloths off tables without moving the china.

plotting to attack Boston or losing track of money spent in defending New York's frontiers, Van Buren stayed on the good side of Andrew Jackson, who by 1837 had had enough of being president. Jackson handpicked Van Buren as his successor, and the voters said, "Why not?" But it was the last time that any vice president was ever elected to the presidency directly from the vice presidency.

That is about the only distinctive thing about Martin Van Buren's presidency, except for the fact that he refused to annex Texas, which at that time was a separate country. The Texans said, "Well then, the hell with it" and have continued to say it to this very day.

Anyway, Martin Van Buren refuted what Leo Durocher said about nice guys finishing last.

· 9 ·

"The Warrior Sage"

RICHARD M. JOHNSON
vice president under Martin Van Buren, 1837–1841

So far, this country has had three Southern vice presidents named Johnson. Two went on to bigger and better things; the third had done his biggest and best thing before he became vice president. His name was Richard Mentor Johnson, and he killed Tecumseh. Tecumseh was a famous Shawnee Indian chief who scalped a great many people. His name spelled backwards was Hesmucet.

The fad for log cabin origins and frontier exploits was just taking hold in American politics in the early 1800s. Johnson was a real child of the frontier, having been born in Beargrass, Kentucky. The name of this town, a combination of bear grease and bluegrass, was later changed to Louisville, which is a combination of Louis and ville.

Following the traditional pattern of frontier life, Johnson began studying Latin at the age of fifteen. Later, he studied law at Transylvania

University. That's right, Transylvania University. By 1807 he had swapped the relative calm of frontier life for the turbulence of a seat in Congress.[52] He remained a congressman until 1819, taking time out to kill Tecumseh during the War of 1812.

This one dead Indian figured largely in the 1836 political campaign. Martin Van Buren and Johnson were running against the Whigs, who were against Jacksonian Democracy but couldn't agree on what they were for. During the campaign, Van Buren didn't have much to do. Everybody knew he was a friend of Andrew Jackson's, so most of the public relations work focused on Johnson.

His campaign featured a five-act play depicting his killing of Tecumseh, which was a pretty thin plot to hang a drama on.[53] There was also a rousing song called "The Warrior Sage." But what cinched the election was probably Johnson's campaign slogan. It went, "Rumpsey, Dumsey, Colonel Johnson killed Tecumseh." It was as hard to forget as it was to scan, and it did the trick.

When he wasn't killing Indians, Johnson was educating them. He founded Choctaw Academy for this purpose, under the terms of the Treaty of Dancing Rabbit Creek.[54] Like any worthy institution aimed at improving the lot of a minority, Choctaw had its token whites, among them Richard Johnson's nephew. He would have sent his own children, but chances are even the Indians would have snubbed them, for Johnson

---

52. It was turbulent because one of the legs was shorter than the rest and he couldn't find anyone to fix it.

53. The producers brought Washington Irving in to punch up the script, but it closed in New Haven after three performances anyway.

54. "Rumpsey, Dumpsey" was not adopted as the school cheer.

was what might tactfully be described as a bachelor father. He never actually married, but he had a kind of arrangement with a mulatto lady named Julia Chinn, who'd been left to him by his father. Johnson and Julia had two daughters. In all, Johnson had three black mistresses. The second, perhaps to get even for Tecumseh, ran away with an Indian. The third followed Johnson to Washington when he became vice president.

None of this seemed to have an adverse effect on Johnson's political career, which could fairly be described as humdrum. The only time anybody paid any real attention to him before he killed Tecumseh was when he tried to get the mail delivered on Sundays. He thought this would head off the establishment of a state religion, which he felt was inevitable if every postman in the nation was allowed to go to church.

When the 1836 campaign results were in, Van Buren had won handily, but Johnson had failed to gain the necessary majority by one vote. As a result, the choice of vice president went to the Senate for the first and only time in American history. Faced with a choice between Johnson and

Vampire belfry, Transylvania. Also shown are wagon, ram, donkey, two bullocks, and fourteen human figures. How many windows can you find?

the Whigs' candidate, Francis Granger, who'd never killed a famous Indian,[55] the senators chose Johnson.

Once he got into the vice presidency, Johnson set about proving that it was an honorary post. To keep himself busy, he managed a hotel on the side. Judging his performance as vice president, a historian has called him "even less effective than some of his least illustrious predecessors," a statement that leaves little leeway for praise.

Johnson's party in 1840 saw the same thing the historian saw. By that time the Tecumseh bit was wearing thin and the Republicans decided Johnson was a loser. In his place, they nominated nobody. How would *you* like it to be said that your party would rather have nobody in office than have you?

---

55. Though he had hung a mouse on an Onondagan in a bar brawl once.

· 10 ·

"Without a Why or Wherefore"

JOHN TYLER
vice president under William Henry Harrison,
March 4, 1841–April 6, 1841

By 1840, the Indian-killing-log-cabin craze hit an all-time high in the Whigs' presidential campaign. Their presidential candidate, William Henry Harrison, had all the essentials. He lived in a log cabin, wore a coonskin cap, drank hard cider, and was the hero of a battle with the Indians at Tippecanoe.

The campaign is therefore known as The Famous Log Cabin and Hard Cider Campaign. It is famous for the unforgettable slogan, "Tippecanoe and Tyler, Too." It was a colorful campaign. Grown men and little boys rolled enormous balls[56] from town to town, presumably to demon-

---

56. What were they made of? The research doesn't say. Shouldn't someone find out? Maybe it's important.

During the famous Log Cabin and Hard Cider Campaign, grown men and little boys rolled enormous balls from town to town. This view of an enormous ball demonstrates vividly why the services of grown men were required in this exercise.

strate the momentum of the Whigs' popularity. There was also a campaign song that went:

> *What has caused this great commotion, motion, motion*
> *Our country through?*
> *It is the ball a-rolling on for*
> *Tippecanoe and Tyler, too—*
> *Tippecanoe and Tyler, too.*
> *And with them we'll beat little Van, Van, Van,*
> *Oh! Van is a used-up man!*

Throughout the campaign, Harrison did his thing of wearing a coonskin cap and drinking hard cider in public. The Democrats had little going for them this time, not even a vice presidential nominee. So in desperation they attacked the Whigs' vice presidential nominee. John Tyler, the "and Tyler, too" man, was a perfectly nice but comparatively undistinguished former governor, congressman, and senator from Virginia.[57] Tyler, the Democrats declared darkly, was not really a Whig but a pro-Calhoun Democrat. Filled with esprit (and probably hard cider), the Whigs turned out another song, shorter than the first, to show they didn't care a whit what Tyler was:

> *We'll vote for Tyler, therefore,*
> *Without a why or wherefore.*

Because of their appeal to the masses, the Whigs won a landslide victory, racking up 234 electoral votes against 60 for Van Buren, who was,

---

57. This is known as the hat trick.

indeed, a used-up man and not much of a Little Magician any more. On Inauguration Day, President Tippecanoe stood in the cold delivering a speech that went on for two hours. It was the longest inauguration speech in American history and the most fatal. One of the things he promised in the speech was that he would serve only one term. He kept his promise with room to spare. He caught pneumonia from standing talking so long in the cold without his coonskin cap. The doctors tried everything: castor oil, snakeweed root, opium, crude petroleum,[58] and brandy. Exactly one month after his inauguration, Tippecanoe died.

Now the nation was used to vice presidents dropping dead, but this was the first time a president had done it, and nobody was quite sure what to do. It took two days to get the news to Tyler and to bring him back to Washington, during which time the country had no chief executive, the longest period the country has ever gone without one. Nothing awful happened.

A great debate started as to whether Tyler should be acting president or president. Tyler, who was tired of being the tail end of a slogan, decided president. He took the oath, moved into the White House, and made arrangements to collect the full presidential salary.

Once he installed himself in the president's office, he dealt the Whigs a bad surprise. He turned out to be a renegade Democrat, just as the Democrats had claimed he was. That will teach Whigs not to ask whys and wherefores.

One gets the impression he wasn't much of a team man, either. He

---

58. Don't knock it if you haven't tried it.

had no faith in committees, not even in his cabinet. The last straw for the Whigs came when Tyler vetoed two drafts of a bill to establish a national bank. Summoning their party lyricist, they drafted a message saying that all relations between them and the President were finished—it was like one of those divorce notices you see in the personal columns. To emphasize Whig unity, the entire cabinet resigned in a huff, except for Secretary of State Daniel Webster.[59] This was just the beginning. During his four years in office, Tyler went through twenty-three cabinet members. He was a good example of what they mean when they say a good politician never cares whether he's loved or not. In fact, he was almost impeached.

---

59. Webster kept out of huffs. They made him carsick.

· 11 ·

Pennsylvania's
Last Vice President

GEORGE M. DALLAS

vice president under James K. Polk, 1845–1849

A bad poem and a good conscience combined to slide George Mifflin Dallas into the vice presidency in the 1844 election.

The poem may have been penned by the same inspired bard who'd written the Whigs' previous campaign ballads. This time he really had a challenge: fitting Henry Clay and Theodore Frelinghuysen into a hard-hitting lyric. Here is how he resolved it:

> *The country's risin'*
> *For Clay and Frelinghuysen*

Many people believe this poem cost the Whigs the election. They should have realized that Frelinghuysen is just about the only other word in the English language besides Orange that doesn't have a rhyme.

The good conscience was the property of one Silas Wright, a senator from New York who would have become vice president without it, as so many other men did.

In 1844, the big question was whether or not to bring Texas into the Union. There were lots of arguments pro and con, mostly concerned with how many slaves this would add to the population. There was no general agreement on annexation until somebody figured out the business advantages, which were considerable.[60]

James K. Polk was a man of modest ambition; like Calhoun, he would have been happy to be vice president. Instead, he turned out to be the original dark horse candidate for the presidency.[61] Almost nobody except his immediate family had ever heard of Polk until the Democrats nominated him for president on the ninth ballot of the 1844 convention.[62]

This accomplished, they scouted around for someone to round out their ticket. Since Polk was for the annexation of Texas, the Democrats chose Seantor Wright, who was against it, to run for the vice presidency. This, they reasoned, would give them a ticket with something for everyone. That's when Wright's conscience went off. He said it would be silly to have opponents on such a burning question running as a team.

So the Democrats nominated George Mifflin Dallas, a former Philadelphia lawyer who was much in favor of annexation. In fact, the city of

---

60. Also, a discouraging word seldom was heard there. A lot of people look for that sort of thing when they're thinking of annexing a state.

61. What is the derivation of the term "dark horse"? Turn this page upside down for the answer.

62. You didn't really hold the page upside down, did you?

Dark horse.

Dallas was named for George by Texans grateful to him for helping them get into the Union.

The election itself was not a very exciting one compared to the last—no rolling of big balls made of some unknown substance or other gimmicks. Just straight-ahead politics. The Whigs, who never seemed to learn anything, thought up another catchy slogan: "Who the hell is Polk?"[63] Polk was the candidate who won the election, is who the hell.

Dallas had had a colorful career up to that point. A member of the class of 1810 at Princeton, he was elected mayor of Philadelphia, and President Martin Van Buren sent him off to serve as minister to Russia in 1837. Dallas found Moscow cold and boring[64] and asked to be recalled. On reflection, maybe Dallas hadn't had such a colorful career up to that point after all.

Anyway, he was very loyal to President Polk. On one occasion, he was called upon to break a tie vote on a bill to lower tariffs. Since Polk wanted the bill passed, Dallas voted for it even though nobody in Dallas's home state, Pennsylvania, was in favor of it. Pennsylvanians were really burned up and begged the Lord to deliver them from any more home-grown vice presidents. They got their wish: to date there has not been another Pennsylvanian nominated to the vice presidency by a major political party.

Dallas's term as vice president was spiced up by the fact that he presided over the Senate during the Mexican War. The United States

---

63. They really did. You can look it up.
64. Moscow found Dallas the same way.

Army really outdid itself, capturing Monterrey, Buena Vista, and even Mexico City. The victory celebration was held in the Halls of Montezuma so that the Marine Hymn could have a catchy first line. Its second line comes from a police action initiated by Thomas Jefferson against the pirates of Tripoli.

· 12 ·

A Yankee to Balance the Ticket

MILLARD FILLMORE
*vice president under Zachary Taylor,
March 5, 1849–July 10, 1850*

By the time the 1848 conventions rolled around, the Whigs were waiting in the wings with a real winner: Zachary Taylor. They even had a half-way decent slogan in Taylor's nickname, "Old Rough and Ready." Old R&R was, as you may have guessed, a war hero, having captured several cities from the Mexicans in the recent war. His political credentials were impeccable: he'd never voted, so nobody could say anything bad about his record.

Since Taylor came from Louisiana, the Whigs needed a Yankee to balance the ticket. About the only one they knew was Millard Fillmore, the state comptroller for New York, so they nominated him. Luckily, former President Martin Van Buren had founded a splinter party called the Free Soilers. Contrary to what it sounds like, the Free Soilers were not

Whig (whith whaves).

advocating giving dirt away. They were opposed to spreading slavery to new territories. In other words, the soil of those territories should be free.[65] By taking votes away from the Democratic candidate, a chap named Lewis Cass, the Free Soilers swung the election to Taylor, who was not sure how he felt about this and a lot of other things, and his unknown comptroller, Fillmore.

As vice president, Fillmore had little to do but listen to the debate that was raging about California, which was one of the United States's prizes for winning the Mexican War. Some Californians didn't even want to be part of the Union; they went ahead and set up their own Bear Flag Republic. The United States government didn't seem to notice. Congress was too busy trying to decide whether California should be admitted as a free state or a slave state. The hitch was that the Californians themselves had adopted a territorial constitution prohibiting the sale or use of slaves. Old Rough and Ready, despite his Southern upbringing, was for admission.[66] A lot of others weren't.

Henry Clay, a persuasive talker from Kentucky, came up with a fiendishly complicated formula for a compromise. It gave everybody something to complain about, and nobody seemed to have a better idea.

The debate headed for a tie, which gave Fillmore something to sink his teeth into for the first time since becoming vice president. His mind made up, he set off for the White House to tell the President that he was going to vote in favor of the compromise. Much as he disliked the notion of slavery—and some aspects of the compromise promoted it—he be-

---

65. Keep your eye on this issue. It's going to turn into the Civil War.
66. He'd tried a slave once, but it didn't do anything for him.

lieved the compromise would save the Union. How could he know, as he headed down Pennsylvania Avenue, that he would not only break the tie but would sign the compromise bill into law as president of the United States?

Here's what happened. On the Fourth of July, Old Rough and Ready turned out with the rest of the population to celebrate Independence Day. It was very hot, so he drank a lot of water and ate a whole bag of cherries. Still thirsty, he washed the cherries down with an iced milk. Almost immediately, he doubled up in agony and was carted off to be examined by the best physicians around. First they thought it was cholera, then typhus, then something called bilious remittant fever. As they argued away, old Zack breathed his last, making way for Millard Fillmore to become one of the least prepossessing presidents the country has ever had.

Everyone knows you *never, never, never* wash cherries down with iced milk.

· 13 ·

Too Good to Last

WILLIAM KING
*vice president under Franklin Pierce,
March 4, 1853–April 18, 1853*

Next time you're at a cocktail party ask someone, "Who is the only United States vice president ever to take the oath of office in Havana, Cuba?" No one will know it is William Rufus Devane King. They may not care, but they definitely will not know.

Right after the election, which he and Franklin Pierce won from the Whigs, King's tuberculosis took a turn for the worse, and he went to Cuba to recuperate.[67] In view of the circumstances, the Senate passed a special law allowing him to be sworn into office in Havana. Little more than a month later, in April, 1853, King returned to King's Bend, his Alabama plantation, and died the following day.

67. This was before Castro.

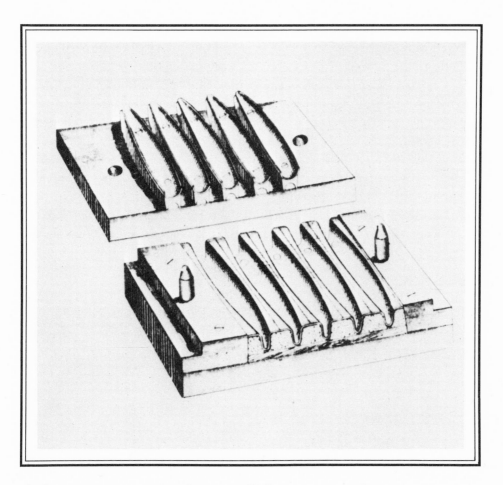

A future vice president will have something to say about the country's need for a good 5 cent cigar. These cigar molds are for bad 6 cent cigars. William King liked them.

It figures, doesn't it? King was a man of skill and experience. He'd traveled abroad extensively, serving diplomatic missions in Naples, St. Petersburg, and Paris. He was one of Alabama's first senators and had served almost three decades in the United States Senate. When Fillmore became president, King was president pro tem of the Senate. He had all the qualifications of a really smashing vice president. Hell, he had all the qualifications of a really smashing *president*![68] Obviously, he was too good to last.

After King's death, the country got along very well without any vice president until the next election. Counting the time that Millard Fillmore was president,[69] the vice presidential vacuum lasted about seven years, the longest rest the country has ever had from vice presidents. And do you know what? Nobody seemed to notice the difference.

---

68. Wouldn't it be fun to say, "We have a King for president"?

69. Come now. Fillmore was forgettable but not *that* forgettable. You read about him in the last chapter.

· 14 ·

The Senate Called Him Traitor

JOHN C. BRECKINRIDGE
vice president under James Buchanan, 1857–1861

John C. Breckinridge was a great public speaker whose gifts of persuasion were such that on one occasion he talked himself right into the army, and on another, right out of the Senate. Other than that, and the fact that he's another one of those graduates of Transylvania U., you can judge how interesting Breckinridge was by the fact that the Encyclopaedia Britannica saw fit to devote only a third as much space to him as it did to Brecknockshire, an inland county in South Wales, which is the very next article in Volume 4.

You can really get *into* Brecknockshire, too. For instance, in 1282 Llewelyn, the last native prince of Wales, fell in a skirmish with the English near Builth. Later, Owain Glyndwr (*see* Glendower, Owen) carried out raids in the area.

One thing is for sure, though. It's easier to pronounce Breckinridge than it is some of those Brecknockshire names. Try Llanwrtyd Wells, Mynydd Epynt, Llynfi, Wysg, and Honddu on your old palate-orooni. Why, they even had a saint yclept Illtud! But we digress.

A Kentuckian whose grandpa had been an advisor to Thomas Jefferson, Breckinridge fell naturally into a political career. His middle name was Cabell, and whenever you hear of a Southerner being named Cabell you can expect pretty good things to come of it, the same as you can from people named Duke or Mellon.[70]

Breckinridge wasn't wildly enthusiastic about the Mexican War, nor did he pay attention when the government called for troops to invade Mexico in 1846. Breckinridge was too busy doing what was closest to his heart: giving speeches.

In 1847, a whole batch of dead Kentuckians who'd been killed fighting with Zachary Taylor at Buena Vista were shipped back to Frankfort, Kentucky, for a first-class military funeral.[71] A crowd of twenty thousand turned out for the ceremonies, at which John C. Breckinridge was the main speaker. The young lawyer got so carried away with his own oratory that he wound up in the army with a major's commission.

Glowing with patriotic fervor, he marched off to Mexico with a company of volunteers, but they arrived too late to gather any laurels.[72] Still, they'd gone, and back in Kentucky that's all anybody cared about. And

---

70. Duke Wayne, Casaba Mellon, etc.

71. In a first-class funeral, you get two free drinks and choice of entrees; in a coach funeral, it's a dollar a drink and you eat what they serve you.

72. The Third Tennessee had gathered them; the Kentuckians had to be satisfied with eucalyptus. But it wasn't the same thing.

Sequoias, like laurels
Breckinridge failed
to bring back,
are members
of the plant family.

Breckinridge could still speak.[73] When Kentucky's number-one orator, Henry Clay, died, Breckinridge was called upon to speak at the funeral. That sort of thing gets noticed.

As a natural successor to Clay, Breckinridge rose rapidly, and at thirty-six he was the youngest person ever to become vice president. He had run on the Democratic ticket with James Buchanan, a reformed Federalist from Pennsylvania.

Like many another smooth talker before him, John Cabell Breckinridge loathed having to sit and listen to everybody else speaking. He was vastly relieved when his home state voted him a term as senator. In fact, because his vice presidential term still had two more years to run, Kentucky voters voted to let his term as senator begin at his convenience. Wasn't that nice?

He would have become a senator on March 4, 1861. But remember that Civil War we said was coming? Well, it came, and the election of 1860 was what did it. If we go into the issues we'll be here all day, so can we just say it was about slavery and let it go at that?

At any rate, the 1860 Democratic Convention was *divisa in duas partes,* as one might say, and the Southern half picked Breckinridge as its presidential candidate.

When the Civil War broke out, Kentucky declared its neutrality, but Breckinridge believed that as long as he was living in Washington this did not include him. His vice presidential term had ended, and he was now a senator. He made one of those speeches of his, and in it he made

---

73. Bet *he* could pronounce Llanwrtyd Wells, Mynydd Epynt, and Llynfi.

no bones about what he thought of Mr. Lincoln's military program. The folks back in Kentucky were trying to be neutral, so the speech embarrassed them. A grand jury in Frankfort indicted him for treason, and the Senate called him a traitor and threw him out.

He packed up and went South to become a Confederate general. He defeated General Franz Sigel—remember Franz Sigel?—at Newmarket, Virginia, and toward the end of the war served as the Confederate secretary of war. At the close of hostilities he fled to England via Florida and Cuba[74] for a self-imposed exile of three years. Eventually he came back and died.

---

74. Since then, direct service has been inaugurated between Kentucky and England.

· 15 ·

A Renegade Democrat

HANNIBAL HAMLIN
vice president under Abraham Lincoln, 1861–1865

Everybody's heard of Abraham Lincoln, but who remembers Hannibal Hamlin? Here's a clue: he was vice president of the United States during Lincoln's first term.

Hamlin was a renegade Democrat, which means that he was against Whigs and Federalists, who were going out of style anyhow. And he was for abolition. In his political prime, Hamlin had been governor of Maine and had also served the Pine Tree State in the Senate. In fact, he bounced in and out of the Senate like a ping-pong ball.

Hamlin was the product of a respectable New England family whose fortunes were reversed during his youth. Too poor to go to college,[75] he

---

75. And he'd so much had his heart set on Transylvania, too, poor devil!

studied law instead and became a Jacksonian Democrat. He was sort of against slavery but considered it beyond the reach of legislation.[76]

Hamlin made his first trip to the United States Senate in 1848, when the anti-slavery wing of the Democratic party elected him to fill the term of a senator who'd died. There's always something a little sleazy about getting into office that way, so in the next election he ran and won a term of his own. Then he switched to the Republican party to get himself elected governor of Maine, and he won hands down.[77] Now here's where the bouncing began.

Hamlin quit the Senate on January 7, 1857, to serve as governor. Then a month later he resigned as governor to return to the Senate. He resigned from the Senate again in January, 1861, to be Abe Lincoln's vice president. Then, after serving in that position, he returned to the Senate in 1869. There, until 1881, he found surcease from all that tortured bouncing.

During Hamlin's term as vice president, the Great Emancipator didn't give him much to do, not even a few subsidiary emancipations. Hamlin tried to attract some attention by differing with Lincoln on a number of issues, but since everybody else was differing with Lincoln on a number of issues at the same time, the President was totally oblivious to Hamlin's gambit.

The second time around Hamlin was dumped from the ticket because, since Maine was for Lincoln anyway, Hamlin wasn't even very good vote bait. Not much else is known about Hannibal Hamlin, except that he smoked and played cards and was supposed to be a teetotaler. We

---

76. Today that position is known as Zoroastrianism.
77. At least, that's how they found him when they came to tell him the news.

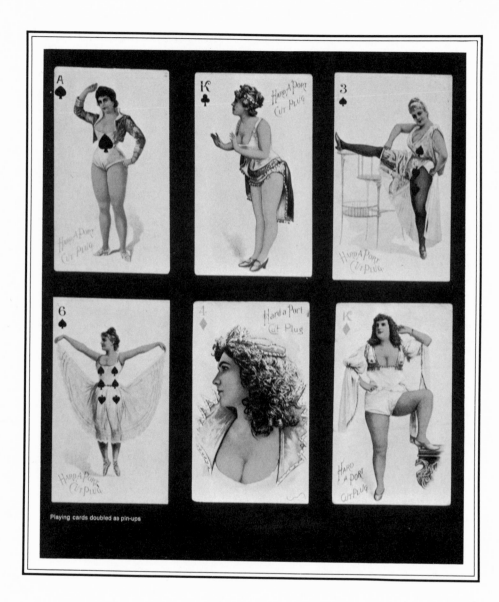

Playing cards doubled as pin-ups

say "supposed" because when Andrew Johnson needed a drink at the wrong time, Hamlin got it for him. As there was never a right time for Johnson to need a drink, the consequences were dire, as you shall soon see if you're good little boys and girls.

Hamlin was also the third vice president to die on the Fourth of July.[78]

---

78. Apparently, morticians gave you a special deal if you could pull that off, and a lot of officeholders took advantage of it.

Hannibal Hamlin was a teetotaler, but he smoked a lot, and he enjoyed a friendly game of cards.

· 16 ·

"Andy Ain't a Drunkard"

ANDREW JOHNSON
*vice president under Abraham Lincoln,
March 4–April 15, 1865*

Andrew Johnson had observed how Hannibal Hamlin had practically disappeared in Abraham Lincoln's shadow, and he was determined to be noticed even though he *had* been elected vice president. To insure this, he showed up drunk at the inauguration.

Actually, it was Abraham Lincoln's fault. Andrew Johnson didn't want to go to the inauguration in the first place. He'd been sick with typhoid fever, and you know how shaky you can feel after a bout with that. But Lincoln insisted. The night before the inauguration Johnson went out drinking with the boys, and he woke up on the big morning with a head that felt like a Shiloh cannonball. How was he going to get through a long, boring ceremony without throwing up or having a sick headache?

So he asked Hannibal Hamlin, who was standing by, to get him something to ease the pain. Tut-tutting slightly, but not unduly, Hamlin fetched a bottle of whiskey and Johnson had at it. By the time he got to the reviewing stand, the ceremony was starting to look pretty good.

Without waiting to be sworn in, Johnson launched right into an unprepared but extremely moving speech. He admitted he knew nothing about parliamentary procedure (which is, after all, about all a vice president has to know), and went on to insist he had none of the requisites for the office. Then, not content with the job he'd done on himself, he moved on to the members of the cabinet, criticizing them one by one in minute detail.

Abraham Lincoln, who was not used to being upstaged this way, sat through Johnson's speech staring at his shoes. Lincoln had written a Major Speech for the occasion but had a distinct feeling that nobody was going to pay much attention to it after Johnson's performance, and he was right. The next day, the newspapers were full of the vice president's inebriated pronouncements, and hardly a word was said about Lincoln's Major Speech.

Johnson got himself noticed, all right. Practically the same day as the inauguration the Senate passed a resolution banning liquor from its wing of the capitol building. It seems like a dumb ban, though. If Andrew Johnson couldn't get a drink from a senator, he could always cross over to the House of Representatives, where there were big supplies.

A poem was written to immortalize the event:

Oh, was it not a glorious sight,
To see the crowd of black and white,
As well as Andy Johnson tight,
At the inauguration.

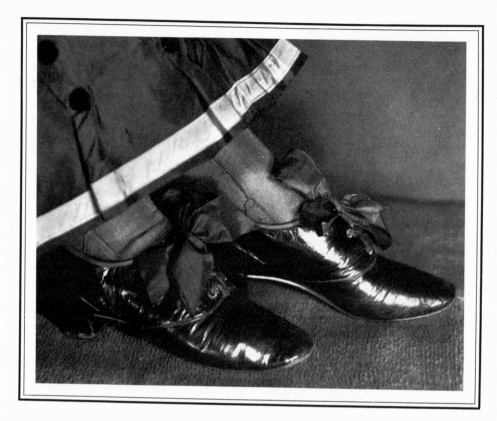

Abraham Lincoln was not
really staring at his own shoes;
he was staring at the shoes and
ankles of the wife of a Cabinet
member down the row a piece.

In view of all that had happened, Lincoln was pretty big about the whole thing. After the inauguration, pressed for a comment, he said simply, "Andy ain't a drunkard."[79]

Fortunately for Andrew Johnson, George Atzerodt[80] *was* a drunkard. Atzerodt was the man given the job of assassinating Andrew Johnson while John Wilkes Booth was taking care of Abraham Lincoln. The assignment was clearly too much for Atzerodt. When the time came to kill Johnson, Atzerodt was out pub-crawling trying to bolster his nerve. Booth was a nut, which is a big plus for assassins, and he quavered not when it came time to kill Lincoln.

As soon as he became president, Johnson gave up public drinking and tried to carry on where Lincoln had left off. Being a Southerner, he wanted to make post-war Reconstruction as painless as possible for his people. But a radical element in Congress was out for rebel blood; if it was up to those fire-eaters the South would be reconstructed along the lines of the Sahara Desert.

So Johnson's enemies claimed he was soft on the South, and to really hurt the guy they revived an old rumor to the effect that Johnson had been in on the plot to kill Lincoln. The basis of this story was that John Wilkes Booth stopped by Johnson's hotel on his way to the Ford Theatre to kill Mr. Lincoln and left a note for Johnson.[81]

A movement to have Johnson impeached got underway, a real first

---

79. Kind of makes you wonder if he really wrote the Gettysburg Address, doesn't it?

80. Pronounced Fotheringay.

81. It does sound pretty suspicious, you have to admit.

in American history. It was a verrry touchy business. But when it came right down to a vote, thirty-five senators were for it and nineteen were against it, which was one less than the two-thirds majority you must have to get rid of a president.

Nonetheless, it takes a lot of the fun out of being president when you know thirty-five senators are that down on you. Poor old Johnson didn't have much shine left on him by this time; the rest of his term was more like a sentence.

All this just served to solidify the conviction that the vice presidency was the first stop on the road to nowhere. Johnson probably would have been happier and better off if he'd never learned to read. He didn't, you know, until he married Eliza McCardle. Then he considered himself ready to go into politics.

· 17 ·

The Great $1000
Campaign Contribution

SCHUYLER COLFAX

vice president under Ulysses S. Grant, 1869–1873

One of the politer nicknames attached to Ulysses S. Grant was "Useless." He was a fine general but a rotten president,[82] and the only reason he got elected president was because he was more famous than anybody else in the country. Grant's first vice president, Schuyler Colfax, was in worse shape; he hadn't even been a fine general.

Colfax did have a nicer nickname than Grant, though. He was called "Smiler" because he smiled a lot. What he smiled about mostly was all the money he was making on the side by participating in the kind of

---

82. Historians have recently reexamined Grant as a president and concluded that he was just as rotten as they'd thought.

business deal that is called a scandal as soon as anybody hears about it. This particular scandal had to do with railroads.[83]

Now that California was a state and gold had been discovered in it, the United States government wanted a railroad to go there. Two established companies, the Central Pacific and the Union Pacific, agreed to build the transcontinental line, the first working east, the other west. The government promised to pay for everything. It also gave the two companies 23 million acres of land so that the track could make an occasional loop or figure eight to relieve the monotony of traveling in a dull straight line.

The trouble was, the government didn't have the faintest notion of how much it cost to build a railroad, while the people in charge of the scandal did. Right away they set up a dummy corporation called Crédit Mobilier to receive contracts for the railroad's construction.

By a miracle of engineering and some very good guesses, the transcontinental railroad was completed at Promontory, Utah, in May, 1869, and a golden spike was driven to hold the two pieces of track together. Their mission accomplished, the Crédit Mobilier folks sent the United States an invoice for $173 million for a job that had cost them a mere $83

---

83. Most of our scandals have had to do with railroads. There's just something about them.

All sorts of nails and spikes, including one golden one, were used in the construction of the transcontinental railroad, a very profitable pie in which Colfax had his thumb up to his elbow.

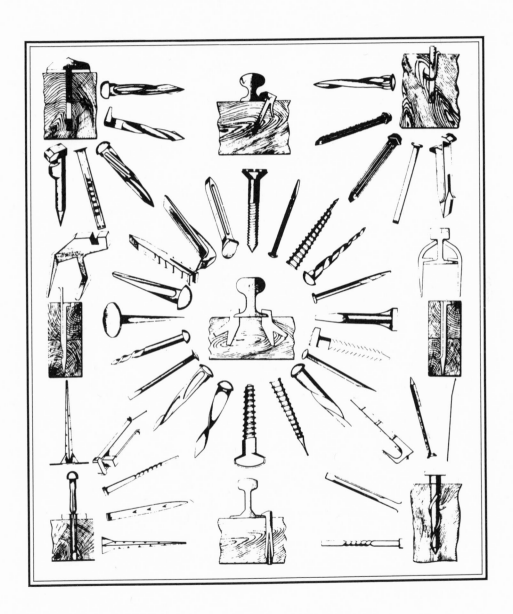

million. The plan was to split the difference; that is, as soon as the government blew its top when it opened the bill on Monday morning, the dummy corporation was prepared to say, "Okay, if that's the way you're going to be about it, give us $128 million and we'll forget the rest." A number of senators and representatives were up for kickbacks if they voted for that compromise. Knavery will out, however, and the scandal began to leak when people got greedy.

One of the top promoters of the scheme, a congressman himself, had tried to pave the way for better understanding by passing out stock and money (or "dividends," as they were called) to other government officials. When the story finally broke, the congressman told an investigating committee that Vice President Colfax, among others, had received $1200 worth of dividends from him.

By a remarkable coincidence, the vice president's bank had recorded a deposit of $1200 cash on the very day the congressman claimed to have paid Colfax his dividend. But Smiler said he could explain.

He was opening his mail one morning, he declared, and a $1000 bill floated out of an envelope: a campaign contribution, he assumed. Unfortunately, the person who sent it had long since died and the envelope had been thrown away. But . . . what about the other $200? Colfax didn't even bother to explain it.[84]

Oddly enough, nobody believed him. There was some talk of impeachment, but since his term was almost up he was allowed to pass uncensured. He was scheduled to be dropped from the Republican ticket,

---

84. Maybe it was a $1200 bill.

anyhow. Grant had had a feeling Colfax was gunning for his job, so he dumped him from the 1872 ticket, which was still two years away.

Colfax, who started out earning an honest living as a journalist, had served creditably in the House of Representatives from 1855 to 1868, when his good luck changed and he got elected with Grant. It was just one more good example of the vice presidency ruining a perfectly adequate man.

· 18 ·

The Cobbler of Natick

HENRY WILSON
vice president under Ulysses S. Grant,
1873–November 23, 1875

In 1872, scouting around for a candidate as famous as Useless Grant, the Democrats nominated Horace Greeley, the newspaper editor who was famous for telling young men to go West. So popular was Greeley's saying that he might have won the election had it not been for his running mate, a Missourian named B. Gratz Brown, whose campaign drinking won him the nickname of "Boozy Gratz."[85] Boozy cleared the way for a Republican victory by getting pie-eyed at Yale and drunkenly haranguing the East and all the people in it, including Yalies.

Oh, it was a great era for nicknames! Grant's new vice president,

---

85. B. Gratz Brown was so ashamed of his first name that he preferred to be called by his middle one.

Horace Greeley's running mate, B. Gratz Brown, cleared the way for a Republican victory by getting stoned at Yale, a feat which attracted more notice in 1872 than it would today.

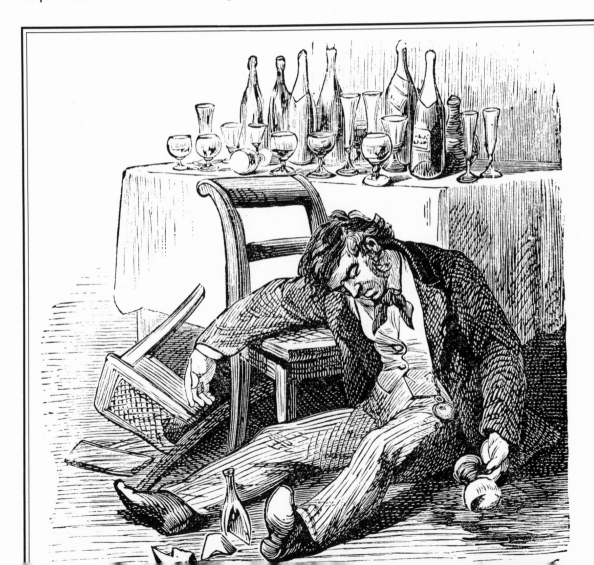

Henry Wilson, was known as the "Cobbler of Natick" because he had once cobbled in that Massachusetts town.[86] In the intervening years, he'd been a manufacturer, newspaper editor, and United States senator, but to a public hungry for common names he remained a cobbler.

Actually, Henry Wilson's original name was Jeremiah Jones Colbath. His father worked in a sawmill, and the family was so poor that Jeremiah was indentured to a neighboring farmer at the age of ten. For his twenty-first birthday, which marked the end of his indenture, he received six sheep and a yoke of oxen, which he sold for $85. He also had his name legally changed to Henry Wilson, which is sort of a shame. Think what the hungry public could have done with Colbath.

With the acquisition of a new name, Henry Wilson felt a burning desire to travel and see the world. So he walked one hundred miles to Natick, where he hired himself to a man who agreed to teach him how to make brogans. During this period, Wilson read a lot and joined the Natick Debating Society.[87] He also had his first vacation.[88]

Understandably worn out after more than a decade of nothing but work, work, work, Wilson journeyed to Virginia and Washington, D.C., where he visited all the best slave markets.[89] He became an emancipationist.

After a brief period of study in New Hampshire, Wilson returned to

---

86. Andrew Johnson was a tailor before Eliza McCardle taught him to read.
87. The subject of brogans dominated their debates. These were very rustic people, remember.
88. He'd given his awl to shoes.
89. This occasioned him to tell the Natick Debating Society upon returning, "When you've seen one slave market, you've seen them all."

Natick and became a shoe manufacturer. For ten years he went at it hammer and tongs to earn enough money to go into politics. He helped found the Free Soil party and later joined the Know Nothings.[90] From the Know Nothings, Wilson settled down as a Republican, and not a moment too soon, either, for Grant tapped him for the vice presidency.

Wilson almost got caught in the same scandal that sank Smiler Colfax. The scandal broke during the election campaign, and it turned out that Wilson, too, had bought some shares in the Crédit Mobilier corporation. But he returned them before the newspapers got hold of the story, so his escutcheon was only a wee bit blotched and he was elected to the vice presidency.

As vice president, Wilson fared no better than most. He had served less than three years of his term when he suffered a paralyzing stroke while presiding over the Senate. He was carried to the vice president's room, where he died twelve days later.[91]

───────────

90. The origin of whose name is fascinating.
91. Had they carried him to some other room, he'd have lived another decade.

· 19 ·

"Who is Wheeler?"

WILLIAM A. WHEELER
vice president under Rutherford B. Hayes, 1877–1881

The 1876 presidential election demonstrated democracy at its most flexible. The winners lost the election, and the losers—Rutherford B. Hayes and William A. Wheeler—became president and vice president of the United States.

This was back in the days when librarians and schoolmarms and anybody else who could read hand-counted the ballots in a back room of the town hall, so returns were slow to arrive at campaign headquarters. Two days after the voting stopped, the Democratic party candidates—Samuel Tilden and Thomas A. Hendricks—were way ahead.

Three Southern states, South Carolina, Florida, and Louisiana, remained to be heard from. So to speed things along, Ulysses S. Grant, the

During his years at the University of
Vermont, Wheeler was so poor he lived on
bread and water for a period of six weeks.

lame duck president and a loyal Republican, sent some Federal troops down to help with the vote-counting. With their help, the Republican electoral board in Louisiana threw out 13,000 votes for Tilden, which made a sizable hole in his 17,000-vote majority in that state. In Florida, where the Democrats had also racked up a big lead, the election board simply declared Hayes the winner.

The only reason there wasn't another Civil War right then and there was that Rutherford B. Hayes had promised the South that if it would let him have this election he would recall the Yankee soldiers and bring about an end to Reconstruction, which had decidedly not reconstructed anything.

The final decision about who was on first was left to a congressional commission of peccable qualifications. The commission was composed of seven Democrats, seven Republicans, and a "neutral" judge who spent the entire night before the big decision hobnobbing with a Republican cabinet member and a Republican senator. To no one's surprise, he cast his vote for Hayes. Nobody called it dirty politics because there was no other kind in those days.

Strange as it may seem, both Hayes and Wheeler were noted for their honesty. Wheeler was one of those poor but honest types who yearned for an education and almost got it. He studied for two years at the University of Vermont,[92] living on bread and water for one particularly barren six-week period.

Finally, his financial difficulties blossomed into impossibilities, so he

---

92. They say the skiing's real good up there.

left college and, like many another impoverished but ambitious youth before him, turned to the law. From lawyer he progressed to bank and railroad manager, and since the shortest route to Congress, as we have seen, is a railroad track, he then ran for congressman and won. In Congress, he established such a reputation for honesty it's a wonder they didn't start calling him "Honest Bill." Outside of his honesty, however, Wheeler's reputation was one of unruffled mediocrity.

Small surprise, then, that when he was first mentioned as a possibility for the vice presidential nomination, Rutherford B. Hayes had to ask, "Who is Wheeler?"

During the campaign, Wheeler played his honesty for all it was worth, stumping for honesty in the administration and also Federal assistance to raise educational standards in the South, which were a problem even then. It's a cinch Wheeler had nothing to do with turning the election in his own favor.

Once Hayes and Wheeler got to know each other, they became fast friends. Wheeler's wife had died the year before the election,[93] so Wheeler spent a good deal of his leisure time at the White House, where a pious atmosphere prevailed despite—or perhaps to atone for—the manner in which its occupants had arrived there. Alcoholic beverages were banned by teetotaler Hayes and his even more teetotal wife, who was known as "Lemonade Lucy," and recreational activities consisted mainly of prayers and hymn-singing sessions.[94]

---

93. Of boredom.
94. Do these people sound as dreadful to you as they do to us?

· 20 ·

"A Barren Nomination"

CHESTER ALAN ARTHUR
vice president under James A. Garfield,
March 4–September 20, 1881

Chester Alan Arthur had a Phi Beta Kappa key and a powerful political friend named Senator Roscoe Conkling, and guess which one helped him to get ahead in politics?

In the 1800s, very few people in politics even knew what a Phi Beta Kappa key was. Everyone, however, knew who Roscoe Conkling was. He was the Godfather of Republican politics in the state of New York. What he said went, and what he said at one point was that Chester Alan Arthur should be appointed collector of the Port of New York.[95]

---

95. The last collector had retired in disgust when the prize of his collection, an 1804 Indian Head penny, slipped out of his hand and rolled off the dock into the harbor.

*A late nineteenth century political machine.
One can easily see why a good mechanic
was needed to keep it running smoothly.*

Up to that time, Arthur had dabbled in politics as a sort of hobby, but he served Conkling well and was regarded, in the words of one writer, as a good mechanic who kept the political machine turning smoothly. Privately, he was a gentleman of some intellectual achievement and a generous host who presided royally at epicurean dinners accompanied by fine wines[96] and superb conversation. He'd won his Phi Beta Kappa key at the age of seventeen and was a teacher before he succumbed to the lure of the law and politics.

At the time of Arthur's appointment to the New York Collector's Office, the Customs House of New York was a veritable nest of political corruption and patronage.

Politely declining to participate in the corruption himself, Arthur went on reading Scott and Thackeray[97] while all around him political hacks of slighter virtue robbed the government blind. Then, on the heels of all those prayers and hymns, came Rutherford Hayes's civil service reforms. In the general housecleaning that took place, Arthur got ousted along with everybody else, so his friend Conkling arranged for him to become Republican state chairman.

At the Republican Convention of 1880, the party divided into two factions: the Stalwarts, who were supposed to be stout, strong, sturdy, brave, resolute, and conservative; and the Half-Breeds, who were not. The former, led by Roscoe Conkling, proved how stout, etc., they were by coming out staunchly (staunchity was another Stalwart virtue) for

---

96. 1869 was a splendid year for claret.
97. Norman Mailer came a little later.

Ulysses S. Grant. Grant had been out of a job for several years and had grown more and more disturbed over the decline of corruption in high places.

The Half-Breeds were united behind James G. Blaine. He had been mixed up in the Crédit Mobilier scandal, too, but his name rhymed with Maine, which is where he was from, and the Half-Breeds figured they could win with slogans if nothing else. Meanwhile, there was James A. Garfield, a congressman from Ohio and more or less of a Half-Breed—let's say, a One-Third-Breed—who'd come to the convention to plump for the candidacy of a dark horse named John Sherman. When the dust died down it was Garfield who turned out to be the dark horse, for he won the presidential nomination (over his own protest, which was ruled out of order).[98]

Conkling was still fuming when Arthur appeared to ask for his permission to run for the vice presidency. His name had been approved by the rest of the New York Stalwarts for the second spot on the ticket. Conkling said no, but Arthur said he would run anyway. Pointing out that the vice presidency was a greater office than he had ever dreamed of attaining, he said, "A barren nomination would be a great honor." Nobody thought much of the Garfield-Arthur team's chances of winning, but win it did.

Garfield had promised to remember the New York Stalwarts when it came to making important appointments, but he didn't. Arthur sided

---

98. A good parliamentarian will hammer these things down the minute he sees them coming.

with Conkling & Company and went so far as to criticize Garfield in public,[99] so he and the President stopped speaking to each other. Then Conkling and another Stalwart senator resigned and headed back to New York, seeking reelection to show that their strength was as the strength of ten because their hearts were stalwart. Like an old fire horse hearing bells, Arthur abandoned Washington for Albany, where he plunged right back into his old mechanic's job, just as if he'd never been elected vice president.

Meanwhile, back in Washington, a religious fanatic named Charles J. Guiteau, who claimed to be an employee of a firm called Jesus Christ & Co., was plotting to kill Garfield because Garfield had failed to appoint him to a diplomatic post in France though Guiteau had put in a lot of time handing out campaign leaflets for Garfield's election.

Step by step, Guiteau proceeded with his plan. First he bought a handsome gun—one that would speak well of his taste when they mounted it in a museum. Then he visited the Washington jail to make sure it lacked no basic comforts. He also practiced marksmanship in a wood near the White House. Finally, his preparations completed, he followed Garfield into Union Station and shot him in the back. Guiteau's marksmanship practice paid off: Garfield died two and a half months later.

While the assassination was going on, Chester Alan Arthur and his old buddy Roscoe Conkling were beating the Albany heat by cruising down the river on a lazy Saturday afternoon. When their boat docked in

---

99. He called him a Renegade Half-Breed.

New York, reporters met them with the news. You can imagine how broken up they were.

Arthur rushed off to to Washington, where he was met with folded arms. He returned to New York, where he remained in seclusion waiting for Garfield to die.

Once he became president, Arthur was a very good president indeed. And would you like to hear about stalwart loyalty? He told Conkling to get lost. Arthur told the Boss he liked him and his boys in the back room and all that, but there were civil service reforms he wanted to get to. Arthur got to them, and it led eventually to the establishment of the Civil Service Commission, which took cynical patronage out of Civil Service and replaced it with stultifying pettiness. In spite of this achievement, the Republicans declined to nominate him for a term of his own. They went with Blaine from Maine, who lost.

· 21 ·

He Left an Enormous Hole

THOMAS A. HENDRICKS
*vice president under Grover Cleveland,
March 4–November 25, 1885*

By 1885 the spectacle of a vice president of the United States dropping dead in office had become a fairly common one, and the nation had taken to greeting these sad occasions with a show of mourning so decorous as to border on indifference. But when the twenty-first vice president, Thomas A. Hendricks, died on November 25, 1885, he left an enormous hole in the administrative web which caused more of a stir than usual.

For almost two weeks after Hendricks died, there was no authorized successor to the presidency; if Grover Cleveland had died, too, the country would have been in a real pickle. A special session of Congress had concluded without bothering to elect either a House Speaker or a presi-

A bird's-eye view of the hole Hendricks left in the administrative web when he died after eight months in office.

dent pro tem for the Senate.[100] The latter post was finally filled on December 7, and Grover Cleveland was allowed out of his room.

Hendricks had a positive knack for timing things badly. He really should have become vice president back in 1876 when he was still in relatively good shape and he and Samuel Tilden won the election. But the Republicans took all those votes away from them down South, remember, so Tilden and Hendricks lost out that time. By the time Hendricks did get to be vice president, he was sixty-five years old and had had two paralytic strokes in five years. Still, he was more fortunate than his former running mate, Tilden, who died before he could ever get another sniff of the White House.

Hendricks never did seem to make much of a first impression. He had run unsuccessfully for the governorship of Indiana twice. Running a third time, he hitched a ride on the Temperance bandwagon and won. He was one of the first Democrats to become governor of a Northern state after the Civil War.

One suspects he would have a hard time winning the Democratic governorship of a Northern state today. During his single term in the United States Senate, he firmly opposed the adoption of the Thirteenth Amendment to the Constitution, the one calling a halt to slavery. He opposed it on the grounds that the Negro was just naturally inferior and no amount of freedom could cure that.

One of the few things people are always writing about Thomas A.

---

100. Next in line was the hat-check girl in the Senate cloakroom.

Hendricks is that he "had little chance to leave his mark on the vice presidential office." Perhaps that is just as well.[101]

Even Hendrick's funeral wasn't all it might have been. He died in his home in Indianapolis, and the President wasn't allowed to go to the services because everybody was worried that something might happen to him on the way. As for Cleveland, he went right on being president for the rest of his term. Then he rested four years and then became president again for another four years.

---

101. If he'd had his way, Negroes today would still be handicapped by poor job and education opportunities and would be esteemed mainly as sports and entertainment figures.

· 22 ·

The Fairest of the Fair

LEVI P. MORTON
vice president under Benjamin Harrison, 1889–1893

This country has had good vice presidents, bad vice presidents, and fair vice presidents. Levi P. Morton was one of the fairest of the fair. In fact, he was so fair he was only allowed to serve one term. No practical politician of either party could bear the thought of four more years of such scrupulous fair-mindedness as Morton displayed.

Loyalty to his friends was another sterling quality of Morton's that kept him from getting ahead in the world. For he was a friend of Roscoe Conkling's, and Conkling, you'll remember, didn't want any friend of his to run for vice president back in 1880. Morton was James Garfield's first choice for running mate, but when Conkling vetoed the idea Morton backed out. Chester A. Arthur, who was loyal, too, but only up to a point, got to be vice president, as we have seen. Wheels within wheels.

Levi Morton was another of those small-town boys who was so poor he couldn't afford to go to college. He was born in Vermont and worked his way south, earning his living for a time as a storekeeper in Hanover, New Hampshire,[102] where he boarded in the house of a Dartmouth professor—the nearest he ever came to a formal education. As he got older and greedier, Morton moved to Boston, where he picked up some useful financial lore,[103] and New York, where he set up a banking firm on Wall Street.

A term in Congress rounded out Morton's political qualifications, which were mainly potfuls of money and Roscoe Conkling's friendship. By the time Garfield asked him to be his vice president, Morton was ripe for bigger pickings.

Offered his choice of consolation prizes, Morton turned down the post of secretary of the navy to accept the job of minister to France. Morton and his wife (his second), packed their potfuls of money and went to France, where they entertained lavishly and just generally enjoyed themselves. About the only official duty Morton had to fulfill during his term was to attend endless ceremonies having to do with France's presentation of the Statue of Liberty to the United States. Morton's only complaint about his French job was that the American legation had its office over a grocer's shop.[104]

Back in the States, Morton ran unsuccessfully for the Senate in 1885 and 1887. Then he was chosen to run for the vice presidency with Benja-

---

102. He wasn't too inclined to cobble brogues in Natick, though.
103. Everybody was reading Adam Smith. Smith is still published regularly, mostly in *New York* magazine.
104. He thought it was infra digs.

min Harrison in 1889. They won handily, for Benjamin Harrison's grandfather was—yes, you guessed it—none other than old Tippecanoe. That old-log-cabin-and-cider-and-big-ball-of-unknown-substance magic still had mileage in it.

When he got to be vice president, Morton's friends were aghast at the way he behaved. Presiding over the Senate, he actually bent over backwards[105] for the sake of the Democratic minority. The Republicans tried everything they could think of to get him out of the way whenever an important vote came up. They told Morton he looked ill and probably should go to Florida for a month or two or maybe even for the duration of his term, but that didn't work. During one particularly crucial debate, Morton even gave up going out for lunch for fear that his fellow Republicans, whom he obviously knew very well, would take advantage of his absence to do the Democrats dirt.

It was the kind of fairness you had to admire, and both sides did. They gave Morton a beautiful, bipartisan banquet at the end of his term. Then the Republicans dropped him from their ticket in favor of somebody they hoped would be a little more on their side.

---

105. Wipe that smirk off your face.

Just before the Statue of Liberty was shipped to America, somebody painted a mustache on her, and Levi Morton had to chisel it off.

· 23 ·

How to Fire Forty Thousand People & Get Ahead in the World

ADLAI E. STEVENSON
vice president under Grover Cleveland, 1893–1897

So far, there have been two Adlai E. Stevensons on the national stage of American politics: the twenty-third vice president of the United States and the one with the hole in his shoe. The first, who was grandfather of the second, once solemnly advised his little grandson never to have anything to do with the vice presidency, which proves that he was a man of great intellect, wit, wisdom, and foresight, just as everybody claims.

The elder Stevenson was a good country lawyer and ardent Democrat from Bloomington, Illinois, who got his feet wet politically by campaigning vigorously for Stephen Douglas against Abraham Lincoln in 1858 and 1860. This is not a very good example of Stevenson's foresight, but it does show what an ardent Democrat he was.

An ardent Democrat like Stevenson needed all the intellect and wit he could muster to make any headway politically, as he happened to live in an area that was densely inhabited by relatively dense Republicans who voted for Stevenson because he was a jolly good fellow. This is how Stevenson got into Congress in 1874 and again in 1878. And it was this gift for making people accept things they had no natural reason to accept that got him even further ahead later on.

By the time Grover Cleveland became president in 1885, Stevenson had become the first assistant postmaster general, so it was his responsibility to fire forty thousand fourth-class Republican postmasters to make room for forty thousand fourth-class Democratic postmasters. Those were the rules of the game in spite of Chester A. Arthur's Civil Service reforms.

It took all the intellect, wit, wisdom, etc., that Stevenson could muster to phrase a dismissal notice that wouldn't hurt anybody's feelings. By the time he was finished, however, the forty thousand Republicans who'd been fired wound up feeling that some kind of honor had been conferred upon them.

That is how it came to pass that when Grover Cleveland made his comeback, Stevenson was picked for the vice presidential spot. As vice president, Stevenson probably came closer to the presidency than his famous grandson ever did, when Grover Cleveland had a secret operation for a growth on the roof of his mouth.

Stevenson also found himself presiding over a Senate that had not long before refused to confirm his nomination to the Supreme Court. But being such a nice man, he didn't take advantage.

He ran for the vice presidency a second time in 1900, as the running mate of William Jennings Bryan, the great orator. It was during this

campaign that Bryan, arguing against the gold standard, gave his famous "Cross of Gold" speech, which made everybody cry but not enough to vote him into the White House.

It is a measure of Stevenson's intellect, wit, wisdom, etc., that his party nominated him to run for the governorship of Illinois in 1908, when he was well into his seventies. He almost won, which was a great achievement considering his age and the density of the Republicans of Illinois.[106]

---

106. Also, Stevenson was not the kind of man to inspire footnotes.

A long-suppressed photograph of the growth on the roof of Grover Cleveland's mouth.

· 24 ·

Politics Was═Were?═ His Recreation

GARRET A. HOBART
vice president under William McKinley,
1897–November 21, 1899

The battle for the presidency in 1896 was called the "Front Porch Campaign," because William McKinley, who was slightly obese and not all that agile, stayed home in Canton, Ohio, receiving visitors on his front porch while his Democratic opponent, William Jennings Bryan, tore around the country making people cry. It indicates a sense of confidence on McKinley's part that was not without foundation.

To say that the business community rallied behind McKinley is not enough. The business community really turned to for McKinley. Workers were warned that factories might be shut if the Democrats won, and manufacturers placed orders that were contingent on a Republican victory. Mark Hanna, the Ohio industrialist and political manipulator who was McKinley's patron but no saint, spent money like a drunken sailor. To nobody's real surprise, the Republicans won.

The main point of contention between the two parties had been that the Republicans wanted to save the Gold Standard and the Democrats wanted to change it to a Silver Standard.[107] Naturally, Garret Augustus Hobart, running with McKinley, was in favor of the Gold Standard. Arguing his cause, he declared, "An honest dollar worth 100 cents everywhere cannot be coined out of 53 cents of silver plus a legislative fiat."

Well said, but of course all wrong. But then Hobart himself said that politics was his recreation and that his main interests were business and law.[108]

A native of Long Branch, New Jersey, Hobart entered Rutgers as a sophomore at the age of sixteen and graduated with honors in mathematics and English three years later. From teaching school, he progressed to the law and branched out into business.[109]

In 1885, Hobart became president of the Passaic Water Company,[110] which had taken over water rights of the Society for Useful Manufactures, an organization that had been founded with the help of Alexander Hamilton.

Hobart had more pies than fingers to put in them. He was the director of a number of banks and at one point in his career was involved in the

---

107. Today we are on the Copper Standard, with plastic coming up fast.
108. We got this from his résumé. His hobbies were chess and classical music, and he had a chauffeur's license.
109. Aren't you the least bit curious as to why he entered Rutgers as a sophomore?
110. Cable address: Passwater.

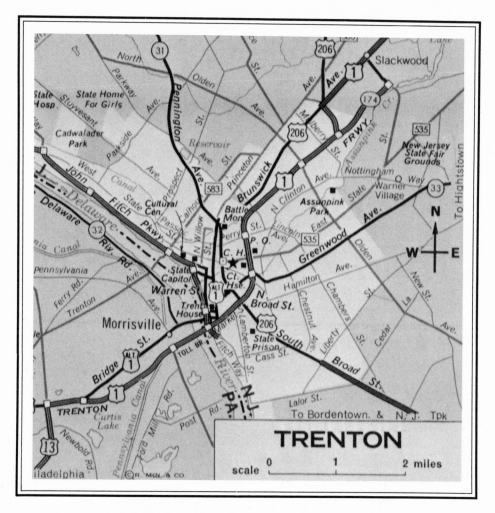

*A map of Trenton, New Jersey, which is
87 miles from Long Branch, New Jersey,
which was Hobart's home town.*

destinies of sixty different business corporations.[111] By 1895, he was very rich and widely regarded as the leading Republican of northern New Jersey.

All these business affairs left Hobart little time for his recreation. He got as far as the state legislature and attended several national conventions as a delegate at large. But he lost the only race he ever ran for the United States Senate, and he probably never would have gotten to Washington without the vice presidential candidacy.

Of Hobart's vice presidential career, Senator Henry Cabot Lodge of Massachusetts said he had "restored the vice presidency to its proper position," a statement doubtless intended as a compliment.

---

111. His record was 45 wins, 12 losses, and 3 ties.

· 25 ·

"That Damned Cowboy"

THEODORE ROOSEVELT
*vice president under William McKinley,
March 4–September 14, 1901*

Theodore Roosevelt was a Harvard-educated warmonger whose prospects soared when he helped mong the Spanish-American War. The war began when the American battleship *Maine* exploded and sank in Havana harbor, right in the middle of a goodwill trip to Cuba.

Some say the Spanish blew the ship up. Others say William Randolph Hearst did it because he needed a war to increase the circulation of his newspapers. Whoever did it, Theodore Roosevelt was right in there screaming for a fight with Spain, and just to show he could put money where his mouth was, he went to play in the war as soon as it was on.

He went to war with a rowdy, ill-disciplined, but interesting group of horsey men who were officially called the First United States Volunteer Cavalry. Unofficially, they were known as the Rough Riders because 1) they rode, and 2) they used rough language, shouting things like "Jolly

Good!" and "Yippee!" and "Remember the *Maine*!"—even in front of the ladies.[112] They had a leader whose name is all but forgotten, so why mention it?

The way things went, everybody thought of the Rough Riders as Teddy Roosevelt's private cavalry, and most people still do.[113] This is because Roosevelt led the Rough Riders in their only war exploit, a charge up San Juan Hill.[114]

Having become a hero, he hurried home to reap his rewards. He didn't even wait for his ship to get to New York; he disembarked at Montauk Point. Almost immediately, a grateful public elected him governor of New York.

That was not his first real job, though. Before the war, Roosevelt had tried his hand at a number of occupations. He'd sat in the New York State Assembly,[115] ranched in North Dakota, run unsuccessfully for mayor of New York, and served on the United States Civil Service Commission and later on the New York Police Board where he tried, poor soul, to clean up the New York Police Department. Just about the time his aptitude for warmongering began to show up, Roosevelt was assistant secretary of the navy under McKinley, whose efforts to resolve the Cuban Crisis without a war prompted Roosevelt to remark that the President had "no more backbone than a chocolate eclair."

Roosevelt's backbone, on the other hand, was as stiff as a stale bagel.

---

112. One of them even said, "Hang it in his ear," but not in front of the ladies.
113. The Swedes are a conspicuous exception.
114. Years later, his political career at an end, he recreated this thrilling historical episode in the Broadway hit *Arsenic and Old Lace*.
115. Of course, anyone can sit in the New York State Assembly as long as he's not rowdy or doesn't stick chewing gum under the seats.

He was a Republican, but a rather odd one. During his term as governor of New York, he came out in favor of putting business corporations under public regulation, which caused every other Republican in the state to break out in hives. By being such an unorthodox Republican, Roosevelt earned himself a lot of enemies in the wrong places. One was Roscoe Conkling's old friend, Thomas C. Platt, who had inherited Conkling's spot as Godfather of New York Republicanism. Another was Mark Hanna, who ran Republican affairs on a national level. Hanna, who was not overly or even underly fond of Roosevelt, referred to him as "that madman." Meanwhile, Platt, trying to think of a way to get Roosevelt out of his hair, endeavored to persuade him to run for the vice presidency, which was the closest thing Platt could think of to burying a man alive. Roosevelt gave it due consideration and wrote Platt a letter saying, "The more I have thought over it, the more I have felt that I would a great deal rather be anything, say professor of history, than Vice President."

All his friends assured him that if he didn't want to be vice president, he didn't have to. All he had to do was steer clear of Philadelphia, where the Republican Convention was being held that year. Well, to make absolutely sure nobody was going to nominate him for the vice presidency behind his back, Roosevelt went directly to Philadelphia. Not only that. As the convention took up the vice presidential question, Roosevelt sneaked into the hall, strode down the middle aisle wearing his Rough Rider hat,[116] and waved to all his friends and enemies. He couldn't have been more conspicuous if he'd pulled in on a golden chariot drawn by

---

116. A large, pink, straw sombrero with "Souvenir of San Juan" and a coconut palm stitched across the crown.

Rehearsing charge up San Juan Hill.

swans, and naturally he won the nomination, which he accepted saying, "I cannot seem to be bigger than my party."

Roosevelt didn't just seem bigger, he was bigger, and as McKinley once again retired to rock out the campaign on his front porch, Roosevelt took to the hustings[117] as the Republicans' answer to William Jennings Bryan. Bryan was a better orator, but Roosevelt waved his arms more, so McKinley and Roosevelt were elected by a comfortable margin.

Once he got to be vice president, Theodore Roosevelt was bored silly with his new "relatively inactive position." He didn't realize that once you've charged up San Juan Hill everything else is apt to seem boring by comparison. He decided to take advantage of the spare time his office afforded by finishing law school.

Meanwhile, a disgruntled anarchist named Leon F. Czolgosz[118] had decided that the United States would be a better place to live without McKinley. Czolgosz[119] went to the Temple of Music in Buffalo, New York, where McKinley was amiably shaking hands with The People, and shot him in the stomach, which was McKinley's primary target area.

When he heard the news, Roosevelt hurried to Buffalo from Vermont, where he'd been attending a conservation meeting that covered everything but the conservation of presidents. Told that McKinley would recover, Roosevelt barreled off to climb the Adirondacks.

He was sitting beside a mountain brook, eating lunch, when word

117. He took to hustings more and more as he got older. It almost ruined him.
118. Have you noticed how disgruntled anarchists are never named Jones or Smith?
119. Pronounced Chalmondeley.

· 128 ·

came on the afternoon of September 13 that McKinley had taken a turn for the worse and was saying good-bye to everybody. Roosevelt charged down the mountain (for a change) and hired the fastest buckboard in town to take him to a special train for Buffalo, but he still missed saying good-bye to McKinley by eleven hours.

With the help of Leon Czolgosz, the forty-two-year-old Roosevelt had become the youngest president in the history of the nation. When Mark Hanna heard of it he said, "That damned cowboy is President of the United States."

In the presidency, Theodore Roosevelt really zoomed into overdrive. He took a firm grasp of the government. In fact, he took a firm grasp of other governments as well. He inaugurated numerous government reforms and paved the way for the construction of the Panama Canal by confiscating a portion of Colombia and calling it the Republic of Panama.[120]

The American people were so pleased with Theodore Roosevelt that they elected him president for a term of his own. In 1908 he retired from office and went home to Long Island to reflect on San Juan Hill and the Panama Canal.[121]

---

120. The Hay-Bunau-Varilla Treaty had a lot to do with it, too.
121. By which time he was hitting the hustings pretty hard.

· 26 ·

The Next=To=Last of the Log Cabin Boys

CHARLES W. FAIRBANKS
vice president under Theodore Roosevelt, 1905–1909

Promises! Promises! Way back when Teddy Roosevelt was at home on the range and only thinking about politics, he voiced the radical notion that the vice president of the United States should be given a seat in the cabinet and a permanent vote in the Senate. But when Roosevelt finally got a vice president of his own, Charles Warren Fairbanks, he dropped the subject like a hot potato.

The reason was simple: Roosevelt despised Fairbanks and Fairbanks despised Roosevelt. It may have had something to do with old school ties. Roosevelt, for all his folksy ways, came from a rich family and had gone to Harvard, while Fairbanks was one of the last of a vanishing breed of log cabin politicians.

One-room log cabin, Republican style.

Fairbanks had a really orthodox log cabin résumé. He'd been born in a one-room log cabin.[122] He worked in the fields in his bare feet, saving his only pair of shoes for the daily one-and-a-half mile hike to school. His parents were both Methodists and Abolitionists, a particularly potent combination of creeds.[123] During his pioneer upbringing, Fairbanks often watched his parents taking care of runaway slaves.

Hungry for education in the best of log cabin traditions, he worked his way through Ohio Wesleyan University, then went on to study law at night while working for the Associated Press during the day. Casting aside his pioneer origins, he moved to Indianapolis, which is where all the money was, and became a rich and famous railway attorney. He was elected to the Senate in 1897 and never practiced law or lived in a log cabin again.

In Washington he became a great friend of McKinley's, which is why, in the mysterious ways of politics, he was nominated as vice president with Theodore Roosevelt, whom he hated. Once the two men were elected, Roosevelt went his way and Fairbanks went his. Fairbanks joined forces with Roosevelt's enemies in Congress to shoot down every program the old Rough Rider sent along. Everybody knew of the Roosevelt-Fairbanks feud. When the President announced plans to take a trip in a submarine, a famous humorist of the time[124] publicly advised him not to set foot under water without taking Fairbanks with him.

---

122. In judging the political value of log cabins, one-roomers are by far the best. Twenty-four rooms mean you're putting on airs.
123. Jewish and Feminist is a pretty good one, too.
124. Calvin Coolidge.

Fairbanks was not much of a vice president even as vice presidents go. His wife had a far more powerful position as president general of the Daughters of the American Revolution. He was, however, responsible for Indiana starting to call herself "The State of Vice Presidents."

Maybe, in all their hunger for education, those Indiana pioneers had skipped arithmetic. True, Indiana had had three vice presidents by now, though Smiler Colfax and his ill-gotten gains weren't anything to boast about. But Massachusetts had contributed an equal number, and New York was surely The State of Vice Presidents if there ever was one, having sent a grand total of nine souls to that exquisite doom.

· 27 ·

A Tool of Revenge

JAMES S. SHERMAN
vice president under William Howard Taft,
1909–October 30, 1912

Three and one half million people voted for James Schoolcraft Sherman for vice president after he died. You would be mistaken if you thought this proved they considered him the best man. All it proves is that three and one half million people think a dead man would serve just as well as a live one in the vice presidency.

Sherman's nomination in the first place was the result of a collective fit of pique on the part of delegates to the 1908 Republican Convention. Although Teddy Roosevelt was ready to step down as president, he was not willing to let the convention bumble along without his advice. His advice was to nominate William Howard Taft.

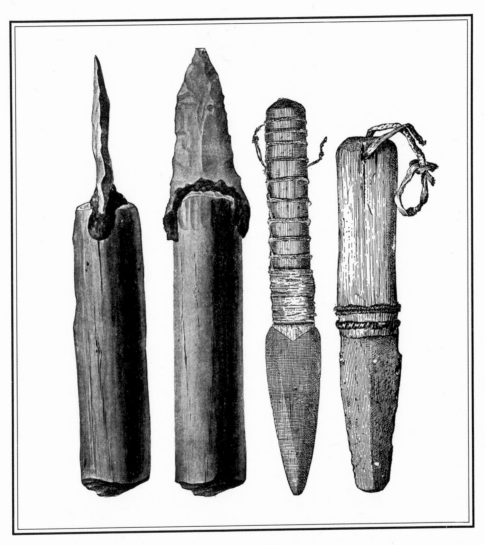

Some of the tools of revenge the disgruntled delegates rejected in favor of Sherman.

Stuck with Taft, the disgruntled delegates[125] cast about for a tool of revenge and found it in James Sherman, whose conservative ways would be bound to annoy Taft, who behind his corpulence and walrus mustache was a progressive. Roosevelt's endorsement of Taft sat well with the electorate, and they voted the ticket in. But as the delegates had foreseen, Taft and his vice president did not get on at all.

James Schoolcraft[126] Sherman was an upstate New York lawyer who took over the family canning business when his father died. This led to banking, and ultimately Sherman became mayor of Utica, from which noble office he proceeded to Congress. His only qualification for the vice presidency was that he was an absolute whiz at parliamentary procedure. But even this rare accomplishment failed to counteract the enormous handicap of his personality conflict with the President.

The two clashed on just about everything. When Taft asked Sherman to serve as liaison between the White House and the House of Representatives, Sherman refused, declaring he was not a "messenger boy."

Poor Taft. Besides putting up with an uppity vice president, he had his old friend Theodore Roosevelt to contend with. Roosevelt was no longer a friend at all, having decided that Taft was letting the side down.

By the time the 1912 convention rolled around, Roosevelt had dusted off his old Rough Rider hat and stormed the hall once more, this time to lead a considerable number of like-minded rebels out of there to form a

---

125. They'd been quite agreeably gruntled till then.
126. It had been Battenburg when his ancestors came over on the ship, but they changed it for obvious reasons.

third party. He called it the Bull Moose Party because, as he was fond of stating, he was strong as a bull moose.[127]

Left to their own devices,[128] the remaining delegates nominated Taft and Sherman again because they couldn't think of a better idea. This gave Sherman another distinction to go with his parliamentary prowess: he was the first vice president since John Calhoun to win a second nomination.

Alas, he died several days before the election, so he never got to know that three and a half million people voted for him anyway. Theodore Roosevelt and his Bull Moose mob really fouled things up for the Republicans, and the Democrats won the election.

---

127. So what? Oxen and elephants and rhinoceroses and hippopotamuses are strong, too.
128. Water clocks, battering rams, and chastity belts among them.

· 28 ·

"Like a Man in a Cataleptic Fit"

THOMAS R. MARSHALL
vice president under Woodrow Wilson, 1913–1921

Thomas Riley Marshall was that rare bird on the American scene, a politician with a sense of humor. He made the American people laugh. Of course, all of our vice presidents have made the American people laugh, but Marshall was different because he did it intentionally.

He found his position as vice president to Woodrow Wilson a rich source of comic inspiration. He said the vice president was "like a man in a cataleptic fit; he cannot speak; he cannot move; he suffers no pain; he is perfectly conscious of all that goes on, but has no part in it." On another occasion, Marshall turned to a policeman who was keeping a protective eye on him. "Your labor is in vain," he told him. "Nobody was ever crazy enough to shoot at a vice president."

Marshall was given the vice presidential nod by a Democratic Convention that was dog-tired after plodding through forty-six ballots to nominate Woodrow Wilson. Wilson, who had been president of Princeton University and governor of New Jersey, was an intellectual, progressive Easterner. The addition to the ticket of a politician with a sense of humor would have insured defeat in ordinary circumstances.[129] But remember, Teddy Roosevelt had taken half the Republicans away to form the Bull Moose Party, which cinched the election for the Democrats.

Actually, Marshall was picked to counteract Wilson's Eastern Intellectual Establishmentarianism.[130] Marshall was a small-town lawyer and philosopher[131] who had risen to become governor of Indiana. Indiana was delighted when Marshall was nominated to the vice presidency because that moved them ahead of Massachusetts in the State of Vice Presidents Sweepstakes.

Marshall's achievements as governor of Indiana were considered progressive in Indiana but spinach in New Jersey, which was fine because there was enough E.I.E. there already. And—oh yes, Marshall helped to swing Indiana's crucial twenty-nine delegate votes to Wilson on that forty-sixth ballot, so as one pol put it, Marshall's nomination to the vice presidency seemed "both wise and practical." Wilson was an intellectual but not *that* intellectual.

Marshall sported a large, gray mustache to compensate for the fact that he was both short and slight. The mustache gave him the feeling of having control of something larger than himself. The first time Marshall

---

129. Look what happened to Nixon in 1960.
130. Hereafter referred to as E.I.E.
131. His *Philosophy of Small Towns*, fifteen pages long, is still considered the final word on the subject.

presided over the Senate he was distressed to discover that his feet didn't touch the floor while he sat in the throne-like Vice President's Chair. This made him feel so insecure, he had the chair replaced with a smaller one. Now he couldn't see over the top of the desk, but at least he felt more secure.

One day when nothing special was being discussed or debated in the Senate, a discontented senator from Kansas named Joe Bristow creaked to his feet and launched into a long, dull speech called "What This Country Needs." Struggling to keep awake, Marshall turned to a nearby aide and uttered quite audibly, "What this country needs is a really good five-cent cigar," which became a Famous Saying on the spot.

Even though he hadn't been born in a log cabin, Marshall found the vice presidency a bit of an economic strain. After all, the job only paid $12,000 a year. To make ends meet, the Vice President toured the country giving lectures that were full of jokes and therefore extremely popular. Following a colleague's advice, he spoke only after collecting his fee.

Some speaking engagements were more successful than others. In New York, facing an audience of wealthy men, Marshall let loose with a tirade against inherited wealth, which caused a magazine of the day to remind him that "little vice presidents should be seen and not heard."

The vice president's chair was not only too big, it was too plain for Marshall's taste, so he substituted this attractive easy throne from his Indiana parlor.

At first, Wilson gave Marshall little to do. But Marshall was characteristically sporting about it. He had decided, he announced, "to acknowledge the insignificant influence of the office; to take it in a good-natured way; to be . . .[132] loyal to my chief and at the same time not to be offensive to my associates." Wilson was so pleased by this reasonable attitude, he chose Marshall as his running mate for a second term.

The Wilson-Marshall combo was running against Charles Evans Hughes and Charles W. Fairbanks, who was trying for a comeback. It was a very close race, and it wasn't until two days after the election that California's electoral vote went to the Democrats. Commenting on the narrowness of the Democratic margin, Marshall said, " 'Tis not so deep as a well nor so wide as a church door, but 'tis enough. 'Twill serve."

During his second term, Marshall really came into his own, drumming up support for the war effort[133] and the Wilson administration. When the war was over and Wilson went to France to see about a peace treaty, Marshall was directed by Wilson to preside over cabinet meetings in his absence. When Wilson returned, Marshall was relieved to be sent back to his vice presidential duties, as he'd been worrying about the constitutionality of his presiding over the cabinet.[134]

Marshall soon had much more serious things to worry about. In the fall of 1919, a very tired Woodrow Wilson set out on a tour of the country to rally the voters behind his pet project, the League of Nations. On

---

132. This is not an ellipsis. Marshall actually said, "to be dot-dot-dot loyal to my chief."
133. It should have been mentioned earlier, but there was a world war going on.
134. This habit of worrying about the constitutionality of things was another trait that set Marshall apart from many politicians of the day.

September 26 he broke down completely and was whisked back to Washington, where he subsequently suffered a cerebral thrombosis which left him just this side of death's door.

As weeks went by and the President showed no signs of bouncing back, people began urging Marshall to take over the presidency on the ground that the President was disabled. On the other hand, Mrs. Wilson and the family doctor insisted this would be bad for Wilson's morale.

Meanwhile, nobody was giving much thought to the nation's morale, which was sinking fast. Marshall would have been glad to take over the presidency if he could be sure that Wilson would stay sick. But he was afraid that the President would suddenly recover and call him a Usurper. This was very delicate: up to that time, the United States had had a lot of things for vice president but never a Usurper.

Oh, it was just one godawful mess. Mrs. Wilson was accused of being a Usurper herself, but she said she was just deciding what was important enough to bother the President with and what wasn't.[135]

Marshall was left holding the fort as best he could. When the king and queen of Belgium came to visit the United States, Marshall took over as official host and entertained the royal couple out of his own salary.

And so it went. The closest Marshall ever came to being president was during a speaking engagement in Atlanta. Someone came to the podium and told him Wilson had died. Marshall asked everybody to pray for him and went back to his hotel. There he found out it was a hoax. Wasn't that a mean thing to do?

---

135. Have you ever heard a better definition of a Usurper?

Wilson never did get much better, but Marshall never got to be president, which is too bad for a lot of reasons. Apparently one of the things Mrs. Wilson saw fit not to bother Woodrow with was the news of how badly debate over the League of Nations was going in the Senate. The League of Nations went down the drain, which it probably wouldn't have if Marshall had had the courage to be a Usurper.

· 29 ·

"I Suppose I'll Have To"

CALVIN COOLIDGE
vice president under Warren G. Harding,
1921–August 3, 1923

By 1920 the log cabin hero had just about gone the way of the dodo, and political leaders were desperately in need of a new gimmick to capture the attention of the electorate. The Republicans did their bit by reviving the dark horse and inventing the Smoke-Filled Room, which has been a staple of the political scene ever since.

What they did was put the names of every obscure politican they could think of in a hat. Then they filled a Chicago hotel room with smoke to make sure that the national chairman couldn't see the names as he groped through the hat. The resultant dark horse candidate was Warren Gamaliel Harding. But Harding was practically a national celebrity compared to the vice presidential selection: Senator Irvine H. Lenroot of Wisconsin.

Dodo, or Dronte, Didus inuptus. *Facsimile of Piso's figure. So what?*

The bosses should have known that while you can shove one candidate down the delegates' throats, they will not swallow two. Back in the convention hall, as someone started a nominating speech for Lenroot, all hell broke loose. Cries of "Coolidge, Coolidge" were heard, and as soon as the speech was over the chairman recognized a delegate from Oregon named Wallace McClamant[136] who was standing on a chair, waving frantically. McClamant nominated Governor Calvin Coolidge of Massachusetts for the vice presidency, and nothing more was ever heard of Irvine H. Lenroot.

Coolidge learned of these developments by telephone in his Boston apartment. Putting his hand over the receiver, he said to his wife, "Nominated for vice president." That wise woman asked in reply, "You're not going to take it, are you?" Coolidge answered, "I suppose I'll have to."

He didn't even say, "Oh boy!" or "Hot Diggity!" But then, Coolidge was never one to go overboard. A man of few words, tight-lipped and dour, his political philosophy was summed up by Walter Lippmann as one of "alert inactivity." He listened a lot, and he spoke very little.

Coolidge's reputation as a word-miser loomed as a challenge to many. A Washington society matron approached the vice president at a party and told him she had bet a friend that she could get him to say more than two words. Coolidge answered, "You lose."

As vice president, Coolidge positively enjoyed his job of presiding over the Senate and insisted he was "entertained and instructed by the

---

136. McClamant had grown a bit paunchier and balder since the last time they met, but the chairman still managed to recognize him.

debates." Well, anyone who can wring entertainment out of a Senate debate is not exactly your live wire.

Warren Gamaliel[137] Harding, on the other hand, drank and played poker and kept a mistress in a coat closet of the White House until the Teapot Dome Scandal[138] caught up with him. Some of Harding's best friends and cabinet members turned out to be members of the scandal: two went to prison, and two more shot themselves.

Harding was so distressed he left town in the summer of 1923 to get away from it all. He went as far as Alaska, which is about as away from it all as you can get, and was just beginning to cheer up. But on the way back he took ill in Seattle and died in San Francisco on August 2. His death has been attributed to food poisoning, bronchopneumonia, a heart ailment, murder, and suicide. Take your pick.

Back East, Calvin Coolidge was vacationing at his father's farm in Plymouth, Vermont, where the modern conveniences did not include a telephone. A telephone operator ten miles away received the message, rode to Plymouth in his[139] Model T, and picked up Miss Florence Cilley, proprietor of the Plymouth General Store, which had the only telephone in town. The two took the news to the Coolidge farm. When he got the message, Coolidge climbed quietly out of bed, put his clothes on,[140] and made ready to assume the presidency.

Nobody thought to ask him how he felt. Perhaps they realized it

137. Pronounced Lenroot.
138. You wouldn't understand it.
139. And how come there are no more male telephone operators, Kate Millett?
140. A very sensible thing to do, considering his prestigious new position.

would be no use. But years later, Coolidge summed up his first reaction: "I thought I could swing it."

Ten months after becoming president by accident, he swung into a presidential campaign of his own with the peppy slogan, "I am for economy. After that, I am for more economy." He practiced what he preached, spending words as if he were about to go bankrupt.

The jazz age was in full bloom, and the country was up to its ears in flaming youth and bathtub gin, so perhaps the people found Coolidge restful. He had no trouble winning a second term.

· 30 ·

"Hell and Maria"

CHARLES G. DAWES
vice president under Calvin Coolidge, 1925–1929

To make up for Silent Cal, the Republicans chose a real loudmouth, Charles G. Dawes, to run for the vice presidency in 1924. Like many another before him, Dawes had done his best work before he became vice president.

A prominent Ohio Republican who had run McKinley's 1896 campaign[141] in Illinois, Dawes went off to World War I a major and returned a brigadier general. During the war, he had been in charge of supply procurement, and when he came back, instead of a shower of ticker tape, he faced a congressional committee anxious to bicker about the price of mules and other wartime purchases which seemed excessive to them.

---

141. With McKinley just sitting there on his porch rocking, it wasn't the most difficult campaign to run.

Dawes erupted. "Hell and Maria, we weren't trying to keep a set of books, we were trying to win a war!" Shades of poor old Daniel Tompkins and his $660,000 discrepancy.

The difference between Tompkins and Dawes was that Dawes got away with it, and a grateful nation immediately began calling him "Hell and Maria" Dawes. When he calmed down, Dawes set to work on a plan for German reparation payments which came to be known as the Dawes Plan and won its author the Nobel Peace Prize.[142]

There was every reason to expect that Cal's cool and Dawes's dash would complement each other and produce a super team for the administration. But Dawes blew it all by counting his presidential favors before they were hatched.

While Coolidge was still trying to decide whether or not to buy a new suit for the inauguration ceremonies, Dawes publicly announced he would not attend cabinet meetings, even if Coolidge urged him to. While confident of his own ability to contribute to such meetings, he said he feared establishing a precedent which would commit the cabinet to having less qualified vice presidents sit in on their meetings at some future date. It was hard to tell if Coolidge was sore about this or not; he kept his lips tight no matter what was going on inside him.[143]

Then Dawes pulled an Andy Johnson by upstaging Coolidge at the inauguration. He didn't show up drunk, but what he did was erupt again, this time attacking the Senate's filibuster rule. Demanding the rule be changed, he roared out a challenge to those "who would dare oppose"

---

142. It was also a root cause of World War II. So much for Nobel Peace Prizes.
143. A lot of psychiatrists will tell you that's very bad.

such a change. Well, just about *every* senator in the land dared oppose it. Dawes's speech was summed up as "brutal and clownish" by one senator. And hardly anyone paid any attention to the neat little speech on government economy that Silent Cal had worked so hard on.

Dawes wasn't even much help to Coolidge in the Senate. He was less help than usual when the vote came up on Coolidge's appointment of Charles Warren as attorney general of the United States. Dawes was taking a nap in the New Willard Hotel when a tie vote on the issue began to shape up. As the vote was being taken, a frantic phone call was put in to the hotel. At the end of the roll call, the vote stood at 40–all,[144] and the halls of the Capitol were dotted with Republican aides on the lookout for the Vice President.

Dawes's dash to the Capitol became, at least for a time, even more famous than his great-great-grandfather's ride with Paul Revere,[145] though one was in a taxi and one on a horse. (Dawes used a taxi.) As Dawes's cab screeched to a halt, the Vice President flung himself out of the back seat and scurried up the steps of the building. He raced down the corridor and burst, panting, into the Senate chamber only to discover that a Democrat who'd originally voted for Warren had been persuaded to switch and there was no longer a tie to break. It was a serious matter, but a lot of people in the land found it extremely amusing anyway. Senator George Norris of Nebraska took to the floor of the Senate with a parody of "Sheridan's Ride," which concluded:

---

144. Also known as "deuce" in parliamentary circles.
145. Look, *we* didn't know anybody had accompanied Paul Revere either!

According to some authorities, including the child pictured here, this is the cab Dawes took for his historic dash to the Capitol. But we don't believe it.

And when his statue is placed on high,
Under the dome of the Capitol sky . . .
Be it said, in letters both bold and bright:
O, Hell an' Maria, he has lost us the fight!

Calvin Coolidge, however, finally cracked an expression, and it was not a grin. As far as he was concerned, Dawes would never be admitted into his inner circle. Dawes, nevertheless, did go on to win the respect of the Senate for skillfully presiding over it, but he never completely lived down his midday dash to the Capitol.

· 31 ·

"He is Dull and Dumb"

CHARLES CURTIS
vice president under Herbert Hoover, 1929–1933

In 1932, the Pulitzer Prize for drama went to the musical *Of Thee I Sing*. The comic gimmick in the plot was a vice president whose name—Alexander Trottlebottom—nobody could remember. He spent most of his time in the park feeding pigeons. Coincidentally, the real vice president in Washington was a man named Charles Curtis.[146]

A contemporary writer described Curtis as a "mediocrity who is as faithful and devoted to his party as he is dull and dumb." Curtis was also a hidebound reactionary from a farm state—Kansas. He was picked for the vice presidency to balance the liberalism of Herbert Hoover, who was nominated for the presidency because of the fine work he'd done to aid

---

146. By an extraordinary coincidence, the father of one of the authors of this book is named Charles Curtis, too. He is not in politics but in women's apparel. Look him up. Maybe he'll give you a discount.

Abandoning the sombrero, Charles Curtis became a compulsive collector of top hats. The sight of a small boy holding a snowball would send Curtis into a palsied rage.

refugees in post-war Europe. That is the way politicians' minds work.

Continued prosperity was Hoover's campaign theme. He talked a lot about a "final triumph over poverty." The way things turned out it was more like a final triumph over prosperity. But never mind. The great refugee-helper and the dull, dumb Kansan swept the country with a final electoral score of 444 to 87 over Al Smith and Joseph T. Robinson.

Up until he became vice president, Charles Curtis, for all his dull dumbness, had been a pretty regular fellow. He'd been a member of the Senate's inner circle, a colorful party stalwart whose sartorial trademark was a large sombrero. His friends called him "Indian" because his mother was a Kaw.[147]

As soon as he was elected, Curtis began putting on airs. No longer a hail-fellow-well-met, he stored his sombrero in a trunk and took to wearing a top hat everywhere but in the bath. He wouldn't let people call him "Indian" any more. He wouldn't even let people call him "Charley" any more.

You have to give Curtis his due. He didn't cater to anybody. Once, when a mixed bag of constituents turned up in his office, he flatly refused to shake hands with the blacks in the group. On another occasion, he described the average voter as "too damn dumb" to fathom the profundities of Republican politics.

Curtis was seventy years old when he became vice president, which may explain if not excuse his cantankerous behavior. And maybe it was all for the good. He was so awful even the party bosses realized they'd have to do better in the future.

---

147. The Kaws were related to the Crows.

· 32 ·

"It Isn't Worth a Pitcher of Warm Spit"

JOHN NANCE GARNER
vice president under Franklin D. Roosevelt,
1933–1941

John Nance Garner was a sickly child who weathered a number of personal calamities, including a rugged frontier upbringing, a case of tuberculosis, and eight years in the vice presidency. When he finally died in 1967, he was ninety-eight-and-a-half-going-on-ninety-nine.

Barring a flash revival of the architectural style, it's safe to say that John Nance Garner will be known as the very last vice president born in a log cabin. This happy event took place on November 22, 1868, in Blossom Prairie, a town in northeast Texas.

People were always telling Garner he couldn't do something, only to stand back and watch him go ahead and do it. When he was only ten, someone told him he wasn't strong enough to pick cotton, so he picked one hundred pounds of the stuff in one day, sold it to buy a mule, and then upped his profit by selling the mule. When he was twenty, Vanderbilt University turned him down because he was insufficiently educated. Vanderbilt changed its mind years later, when Garner had become a Famous Man, and offered him an honorary degree. Garner turned it down.

Like many another American statesman of the nineteenth century, Garner turned to the study of law when he found he couldn't go to college. He became a lawyer at twenty-one.[148] About this time, Garner was advised that he would die if he didn't move to a drier climate, so he shifted his base of operations diagonally across state to the town of Uvalde in southwest Texas. There it was so dry, the only other thriving form of life besides Garner was cactus. There was so much cactus around Uvalde, Garner's friends began calling him "Cactus Jack."[149]

Garner won his political spurs in 1898 with his election to the Texas legislature. He didn't go to Washington until 1902, when he won a seat in Congress with a campaign that took him from one end of his district to the other by every available mode of locomotion—foot, horseback, horse-and-buggy, and stagecoach. He was subsequently reelected to the House of Representatives fifteen times.

When he got to Washington, Cactus Jack made friends with all the right people and learned his parliamentary procedure forwards and backwards,[150] with an eye to becoming Speaker of the House. It was his

---

148. There weren't that many laws to remember then, especially in Blossom Prairie, Texas.
149. It sounded better than "Cactus John" Nance.
150. He was fond of saying, "Order of out you're!"

only ambition in life, but he was handicapped by not being senile, which is a *sine qua non* for that post. Nevertheless, after a twenty-nine-year wait, he realized his dream in 1931 at the age of sixty-three. Sadly, he held the position only a little more than a year before he got siphoned off into the vice presidency.

A master of the art of compromise, Garner did his best work in committee rooms, and he had really bloomed in the Speaker's post. He invited congressmen to "board of education" meetings in his office, where he passed out bourbon and branch water, which he called "striking a blow for liberty." Garner's bourbon paved the way for many a congressional compromise. His patience behind the scenes was apparently inexhaustible. It diminished considerably in the House chamber, though. Garner reached the boiling point during a long, droning debate about the budget. "All those who wish to balance the budget please rise!" he shouted. Everybody rose. "Let the record so note. Let all those who do not wish to balance the budget stand." Not a soul stood up, and the legislation was hustled along.

During one session, Huey Long, who was no friend of Garner's, asked the Speaker what to do if he were half in favor of a bill and half against it. "Get a saw and saw yourself in half," Garner advised him. "That's what you ought to do anyhow."

A still for producing mild porter, stale porter and the like, all of which John Nance Garner considered greasy kid stuff.

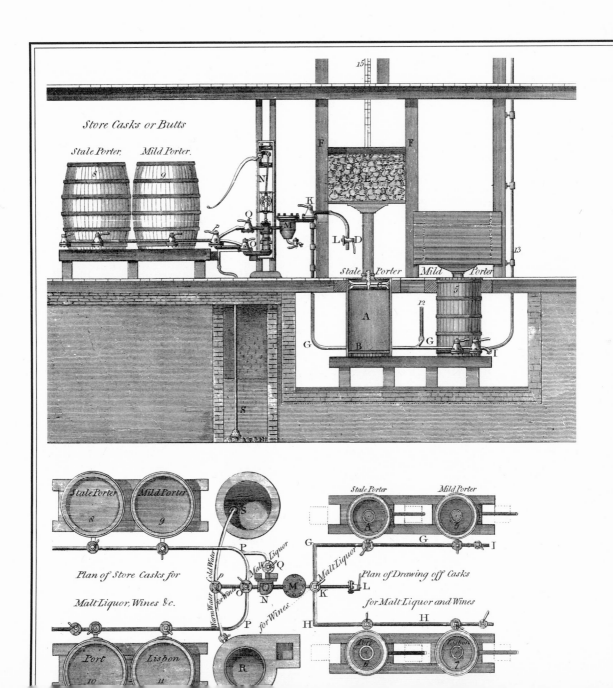

Store Casks or Butts

Stale Porter.　　Mild Porter.

Stale Porter.　Mild Porter

Plan of Store Casks for

Malt Liquor, Wines &c.

Plan of Drawing off Casks

for Malt-Liquor and Wines

Stale Porter　　　Mild Porter

Cold Water for Wines

Warm Water for Wines

Malt Liquor

Malt Liquor

for Wines

Port　　Lisbon

All in all, Garner was doing quite well for a sickly kid from Texas when the Democrats tapped him for the vice presidential nomination in 1932. The Democrats thought Garner would provide just the right philosophical, geographical, and sociological balance for Franklin Delano Roosevelt, who was just another rich Eastern Harvard graduate. But Garner didn't want the job at all.

He reasoned accurately that the job he already had was the second most important in the country. If anything, his estimation of the vice presidential office deteriorated in the ensuing years. Much later, he told another rising Texas politician, Lyndon B. Johnson, that "the vice presidency isn't worth a pitcher of warm spit."[151]

Nevertheless, after the election Garner set out to prove that the vice president could make a contribution. FDR used Garner where he did the most good, as a liaison between Congress and the White House. For his part, Garner treated Roosevelt like a new kid on the block, helping him to figure out which way the congressional wind was blowing.[152]

In 1935, Roosevelt sent Garner to represent the United States at the inauguration of President Quezon of the Philippines. It was the first time a vice president had ever been sent abroad on official business, but it wasn't the last.

Everything was still rosy in 1936, when Roosevelt and Garner won what can only be called a decisive victory over Alf Landon and someone named Colonel Frank Knox. The electoral vote was 523 to 8. Understandably, the victory went to Roosevelt's head.

---

151. This was hyperbole. The vice presidency *is* worth a pitcher of warm spit.
152. You should never stand downwind of Congress.

Emboldened by the election returns, Roosevelt sped forward with plans for more New Deal legislation.[153] To Garner, this meant more bureaus with three initials and more confusion. He urged the President to "let the cattle graze," but Roosevelt was not versed in Western metaphor and ignored Garner's advice. Gradually but inexorably,[154] the two men drew apart.

One of Roosevelt's pet peeves was the United States Supreme Court, which he thought needed an airing. He came up with a plan to add one new, Liberal justice to the court for every justice who was seventy years old, had served at least a decade, and had not yet had the good sense to retire.

Garner, who was approaching his seventieth birthday, thought this was a rotten idea. To show just how rotten an idea he thought it was he stood in the lobby outside the Senate chamber, holding his nose with one hand and giving a thumbs-down sign with the other. It was one of the best things about Garner: you alway knew where he stood.

Up to this time, Roosevelt had been including Garner in cabinet meetings. Now, Roosevelt took to having private sessions with more trusted aides after the formal meeting was over. Garner called these conclaves "prayer meetings."

When FDR began contemplating a third term, Garner almost had apoplexy. "I wouldn't vote for my own brother for a third term," he said, and offered himself as a candidate to show how strongly he opposed this

---

153. Oh yes, there was a Depression on. Sorry to keep forgetting some of these key developments.

154. A few thought it exorable, but they were in the minority.

unprecedented move. The delegates went ahead and drafted Roosevelt anyway. Perhaps they thought Garner, who was now seventy-one, was too old and wouldn't last out a term. Garner lived to see many of them buried.

Garner went back to Texas, where for the next twenty-six years he sat on his front porch gazing at the cactus and spitting occasionally and coming to look more and more like a white-haired iguana with each passing year.

· 33 ·

"A Wild=Eyed Fellow"

HENRY A. WALLACE
vice president under Franklin D. Roosevelt,
1941–1945

Publicly, Franklin Delano Roosevelt carried on like a debutante about seeking a third term. Privately, he had his heart set on a unanimous nomination. The chances of this happening were improved by the fact that the 1940 Democratic Convention city was Chicago, always a good place for accomplishing the delegates' will with a minimum of hassle.

The mayor of Chicago, Ed Kelly, was put in charge of producing a one-ballot show. So he stationed one of his minions, who happened to be the superintendent of sewers,[155] in a small basement room with a microphone wired to the public address system in the hall above. As the pro-

---

155. Traditionally, the mayor of Chicago appoints a special superintendent of sewers just to handle Democratic conventions.

ceedings got underway, delegates were startled to hear a stentorian voice intoning, "America Wants Roosevelt," "We Want Roosevelt," "New Jersey Wants Roosevelt," and similar slogans. Some delegates thought it was God; others said it couldn't be God because Roosevelt was God. At any rate, Roosevelt got his first-ballot nomination for an unprecedented third term as president.

With power to spare, Roosevelt pulled onto his ticket his secretary of agriculture, Henry Agard Wallace, who had had the good sense to declare himself in favor of a third term for Roosevelt as far back as October, 1939. Not everybody—in fact, hardly anybody—was happy with the choice.

The Democratic national chairman, James A. Farley, protested, "The people look on him as a wild-eyed fellow." Many scoffed at this. They would not have done so HAD THEY KNOWN ABOUT THE LETTERS.

To understand THE LETTERS, it is necessary to understand one thing about Henry A. Wallace: his curiosity. A native of Iowa, Wallace was born curious as a cat, and as he grew older he got curiouser and curiouser. In fact, not since Thomas Jefferson had the nation seen a public servant so overloaded with curiosity.

It stood to reason that when a bearded mystic named Nicholas Konstantinovich Roerich[156] told Wallace that he had evidence of the Second Coming of Christ, Wallace believed him. Roerich was a man of wide interests. He had studied art and law in his native St. Petersburg, then had branched out into archaeology, a science he pursued with expeditions to Kashmir, Turkestan, Sikkim, and Tibet.[157]

Roerich's story was convincingly simple: in Central Asia, he had

---

156. Rhymes with Czolgosz.
157. Also Perth Amboy, but there wasn't much shakin' there.

Henry Wallace came from a family of famous agriculturists.

come upon certain Buddhist documents describing a visit Jesus Christ had made to India as a young man. Putting two and two together, Wallace and Roerich arrived at the inevitable conclusion that a Second Coming had just taken or was just about to take place in Central Asia.

Previously, Wallace had made something of a name for himself in the corn field. As a member of a family of famous agriculturalists, Henry took a special interest in corn. In his youth he proved that good-looking corn was less nutritious than ugly corn. He also developed a strain of hybrid corn so that he could market it under the name of HiBred Corn, which he thought was pretty funny. That's midwest corn for you.

Wallace's efforts on behalf of corn brought him to the attention of that great corn fancier Franklin Delano Roosevelt, whose First Coming was just getting underway, and Roosevelt appointed him secretary of agriculture, the same job Henry's father had held under Presidents Harding and Coolidge.

American agriculture was in a bad way when Wallace took over, and he offended a lot of sensibilities by suggesting the slaughter of six million pigs as a partial remedy. In rebuttal, Wallace declared what a tribute it was to the "humanitarian instincts of American people that they sympathize more with little pigs . . . than with full-grown hogs." He went on to suggest, "Perhaps they think that farmers should run a sort of old folks' home for hogs. But we have to think about farmers as well as hogs."

One of the first things Henry Wallace did when he got his hands on the Department of Agriculture was to send his old buddy Nicholas Konstantinovich Roerich off to Mongolia to search for signs of the Second

Coming of Christ. Even Henry Wallace realized how odd this would look on the department budget, so he publicly declared that Roerich was going to look for drought-proof grasses. But whatever you called it, the expedition was a flop.

In the first place, the Mongolians watching Roerich plod around looking for footprints concluded he was a spy. Secondly, the U. S. Treasury Department announced that Roerich hadn't paid his income tax. Finally, Central Asia is a big place, and a Second Coming could happen just about anywhere. So Henry Wallace was forced to wash his hands of the whole affair and turn his attention back to agriculture and the common man, which had supplanted corn in his affections.

About this time, Franklin Roosevelt picked Wallace as his running mate, and THE LETTERS came to light. THE LETTERS were forwarded to newspapers by angry disciples of Roerich who were trying to get even with Wallace for what they considered his shabby treatment of The Master. There was nothing really wrong with THE LETTERS except that they had a kind of mystical tone that wouldn't make much of an impression on your average, down-to-earth voter and might lead seasoned pols like Mayor Ed Kelly to conclude that a heartbeat away from the presidency sat a certifiable nut.

One letter complained of having to attend a senatorial dinner after a hard day. "My eyes did not focus properly," Wallace explained. Then, "I remembered the lovely gift of musk and rose and a pinch of it cleared up my vision like magic." What would the voters think of a vice president who took pinches of musk and rose to make his eyes focus properly? Another letter declares, "I have thought of the new country going forth, to meet the seven stars under the sign of the

three stars. And I have thought of the admonition, 'Await the stones.'"
Hmmm.[158]

It was a smashing example of a man being carried away by his curiosity. As Eleanor Roosevelt put it ever so tactfully, "He was not realistic enough to appreciate how these letters would look to people who did not have the same kind of curiosity." Perhaps he himself realized this belatedly. At any rate, Wallace denied that he'd written the letters, and the newspapers were too scared to print them over his denials, so the country never did get to hear about Henry's hobby before the election.

What they did get to hear afterwards was Henry's concern for the common man. During a particularly evangelical year, Wallace traveled forty thousand miles, gave eighty-eight speeches, and wrote twenty articles and three books on the subject.

As vice president, his star rose quickly.[159] Franklin Delano Roosevelt gave him a lot of important things to do, including running the Economic Defense Board (E.D.B.), which later became the Board of Economic Warfare (B.E.W.). F.D.R. also asked H.A.W. to sit on a committee that decided what the U.S.A. should do about atomic energy. (The A.E.C. finally took charge of it.)

While he was running the B.E.W., Wallace tangled with Secretary of Commerce Jesse H. Jones, who had a board of his own to run, over who

158. Enigmatic at the time, this statement obviously refers to the Rolling Stones —three from seven equal four, not counting the leader—who were just coming into their own in this country in 1965, the year Wallace died. Or, alternately, maybe Wallace *was* a certifiable nut.

159. That still leaves a number of other stars unaccounted for. Damn, it's intriguing!

had access to what strategic resources. Roosevelt settled the argument by disbanding the B.E.W. and turning Wallace out of the executive branch. Roosevelt even resorted to the old ploy of a Goodwill Tour to get Wallace out of his hair for a while.

Landing in Bolivia full of goodwill, Wallace set the Latins to wondering whether or not he might be some kind of god by leaping out of the plane and going straight to a tennis court and playing two sets of tennis. Previous goodwill ambassadors had usually been carried gasping in a litter to their hotels after a few breaths of Bolivia's rarified atmosphere.[160]

Still questing for the common man, Wallace developed a blind spot in regard to the Soviet Union, and he allowed himself to be used by the Communists. He spoke of the U.S.S.R. in glowing terms, which was not as subversive as it sounds because the United States and Russia were allies at the time.[161] Still, the end was in sight for Henry Wallace's vice presidential career, and no amount of musk and rose was going to reverse his downward slide.

As the 1944 convention neared, Roosevelt sent Wallace off to China while he planned for the future. His plans did not include Wallace, but when Wallace returned from the Far East,[162] Roosevelt couldn't bring himself to tell his Vice President he was dropping him from the ticket.

---

160. Bolivia is too poor to afford oxygen. They have to import it from Argentina. In turn, they export nitrogen in the form of fertilizer. Carbon dioxide is no problem.
161. Oops, blew it again. World War II was in progress then.
162. Whatever the official purpose of the visit, you can bet your boots he checked out the Second Coming while there.

Instead, he promised to write Wallace a letter of endorsement. But this didn't mean much, because Roosevelt had also promised to endorse James Byrnes and Harry Truman for the vice presidency.[163]

Wallace decided to go down fighting, and he did. He made a speech seconding Roosevelt's nomination, but if you listened carefully you realized it was a speech for his own. He got the convention organist to play his song, a snappy little number called "Iowa—That's Where the Tall Corn Grows," over and over. He also packed the hall with his supporters, who chanted his name and paraded around the floor until it almost looked as though he was getting somewhere.

What to do? Well, good old Ed Kelly, who was still mayor of Chicago and in charge of the proceedings, suddenly noticed that a fire hazard existed.[164] So he ordered the hall cleared, and by the next day all the starch had gone out of Wallace's campaign and he lost the vice presidency.

To show he was sorry, Roosevelt appointed Wallace secretary of commerce when he got to be president for the fourth time.

---

163. To be fair to FDR, maybe he was contemplating a Troika for that office.
164. Another Chicago tradition is a special fire superintendent for Democratic conventions.

· 34 ·

"A Statesman is Only a Dead Politician"

HARRY S. TRUMAN
*vice president under Franklin D. Roosevelt,
January 20–April 12, 1945*

In the long run, Harry Truman's cultural contributions to the nation may outweigh his political achievements, which are no mean. Who can forget his piano rendition of "The Missouri Waltz"? Or the blow he struck for performing artists when he called a music critic an s.o.b.?

The perspective of history will doubtless endow Truman's cultural gifts with the glow they deserve. Meanwhile, we muddle along thinking of the man from Missouri as a former haberdasher who dropped atom bombs on Japan. It's not fair.

In the first place, though much has been written about Truman's career as a haberdasher, few bother to point out what a bad haberdasher he was. It was partly the breaks. He chose to embark on his haberdash-eryhood on the eve of a great depression. He wound up bankrupt and out of work at the age of thirty-eight. He cast about for something else to do and decided on politics.

Think of it! Nowadays, a man has to be a millionaire just to have the faintest chance of success in politics. In those days—the recession of 1921–22—Truman turned to politics because it was the only job he could find! *O Tempora! O Mores!*

It was not because he hadn't tried other pursuits. Born on a farm in Lamar, Missouri, Truman grew up in Independence. What he really wanted to be was a soldier, but West Point turned him down because of his poor eyesight. He worked as a bank clerk and as a bookeeper. With his father and brother, he helped run a large but unprofitable farm, all the while dreaming of military glory.[165]

He got his wish when World War I broke out and National Guards-man Truman was sent to France, where he rose to the rank of captain, commanding a rowdy bunch of Irishmen[166] from Kansas City. After the war, he realized that everybody was going to need new clothes, so he went into the haberdashery business in Kansas City, where everything was up-to-date.

Fortunately, one of his customers was an old army buddy who was related to Tom Pendergast (who later changed his first name to Boss). When Truman's haberdashery went bust, Pendergast, who ran Kansas, put Truman to work for him in Independence.

---

165. Or maybe it was *millinery* glory. That would account for a lot of things.
166. O'Tempora, O'Mores, and that gang.

Recent photo of Kansas City, indicating everything is up to date.

The boss's support helped Truman reach the U.S. Senate in 1934, but when *Pendergast* went bust, Truman emerged as the Mr. Clean of the Pendergast outfit. While Pendergast and several of his pals went to jail, Truman went on to bigger and better things in Washington.

In Congress he worked his way into the prevailing clique, which meant he got to drink bourbon and branch water with Cactus Jack and his cronies. Truman also saved the taxpayers $15 million as chairman of a committee assigned to watch over the National Defense Program—a stitch here, a tuck there, just like in the old days. So by 1944 Washington newsmen picked him as one of the ten most valuable men in wartime Washington.[167]

Anxious lest the senator from Missouri rise to further eminence, Democratic leaders decided to exalt him to oblivion by putting him up for the vice presidency, to replace Wallace. There were more candidates for the vice presidency in 1944 than there were delegates to the Democratic Convention, and FDR avoided any show of favoritism by assuring each of the aspirants that he was for him. Truman won the nomination mainly because he didn't want it. His wife didn't want it, either.

After accepting the nomination, Truman and his wife were hustled through a pressing crowd by Secret Service men. Sensible Bess Truman, who never, never lost her head, turned to her husband and said humorlessly, "Are we going to have to go through this all the rest of our lives?"

Truman could have been the best vice president ever. The first thing he did after being elected was to start the backstage bourbon flowing

---

167. The other nine sold canned hams on the black market.

again at the Senate, so he had a lot of friends there. Unfortunately, he never had time to get adjusted to his new job. He was vice president less than three months when Roosevelt upped and died in Warm Springs.

Truman almost cried when he heard the news. He told reporters, "Boys, if you ever pray, pray for me now."[168] For weeks he went around telling everybody he wasn't up to the job, until finally Senator Alben W. Barkley pointed out that he was all the president the United States had and he'd better start being a leader or the people would lose confidence in him.

Once he got the hang of it, Truman was an absolutely dandy president. He rebuilt the White House, took over the steel companies, dropped atomic bombs on Japan, fired General Douglas MacArthur, and won a fight with John L. Lewis—all real milestone accomplishments, although they didn't necessarily happen in that order.

Truman enjoyed his spare time, too. He took long, morning walks all over Washington, followed by a panting pack of Secret Service men. He cruised up and down the Potomac, wearing shirts that made everybody look the other way. And he played the piano whenever he saw a movie actress sitting atop one.

Truman's voice was not one of his greatest political assets. It was high-pitched and twangy. And funny, those were almost the very words a Washington music critic used to describe the concert debut of Truman's daughter, Margaret, who wanted to be a singer as badly as her daddy had wanted to be a soldier. Like father, like daughter: he had poor eyesight, she had poor pitch. But as any father will do, Truman refused

---

168. Notice how everybody prays for the president but not for the vice president?

to hear his daughter's clinkers for what they were. He wrote the music critic a short note telling him he was an s.o.b., which the music critic had to look up. It caused a dandy stir on the Hill.

Truman's greatest moment came in 1948 when he fooled pol and pollster alike by beating Thomas E. Dewey in the presidential election while every paper in the country was busily spacing out headlines like "It's President Dewey."

In 1952 he and Bess retired to Independence, where he wrote his memoirs and the people built him a library and admirers and aspiring politicians dropped by, mostly on election eve, to get their pictures taken shaking hands with him. They call him The Elder Statesman, but he doesn't care for that. "A statesman," he once opined, "is only a dead politician."

· 35 ·

The Veep

ALBEN W. BARKLEY

vice president under Harry S. Truman, 1949–1953

Despite a somewhat battered personal appearance and the fact that he was a septuagenarian,[169] Alben W. Barkley was probably the most romantic vice president this country has ever had.

Historical writers, always on a sharp lookout for firsts, are quick to agree that Barkley was the first vice president in the history of the nation to use the Senate podium to write love letters on. He publicly admitted, "I would have tolerated anything, even the most outrageous sort of filibuster, to keep the Senators talking so I could get my love letters written."

The object of all this sentimental scribbling was a widow lady named

169. Having been born under the sign of Septuagenarius.

Jane Hadley who hailed from St. Louis, Missouri.[170] The two met in the summer of 1949 on a boat trip down the Potomac, and for once Washington gossip columnists were right. They'd been linking Barkley's name with every widow in town ever since his first wife died in 1947. This time it was true, and a titillated nation followed the Kentuckian's courtship of the St. Louis woman throughout the summer and fall of 1949. The pair were married in St. Louis in November, and Barkley had racked up another first—two in fact. He was the oldest vice president in American history, and he was the first to get married while serving in that office.

It had taken Barkley long enough to reach the vice presidency. His name had been bandied about as a vice presidential possibility at every Democratic convention since 1928. A lawyer from Kentucky, he'd served in Congress from 1913 to 1927, and during his four subsequent terms in the Senate he'd been majority leader, minority leader, and majority leader as the people kept voting some rascals out and others in.

He reached the semifinals in 1944 when, it will be recalled, Franklin Delano Roosevelt was promising his endorsement to all who wanted to be vice president and several who didn't. By the time Harry Truman was looking for a running mate in 1948, nobody wanted to run with him because they were sure the Republicans would win.

You might say Barkley was the star of the 1948 convention. He was the temporary chairman, keynote speaker, and also chairman of the committee appointed to notify the vice presidential nominee of his nomination, which turned out to be most convenient.

---

170. They could hear her hailing all the way to Jefferson City.

Alben W. Barkley was picked for the vice presidency because he was an expert kisser, as this photograph of an ecstatic kissee attests.

Once nominated, Barkley gave the campaign his all.[171] While Truman gave 'em hell at whistle stops, Barkley barnstormed the country in a chartered plane, giving more than 250 speeches and traveling 150,000 miles to 36 states in the space of six weeks.[172]

The only unhappy person after the election was Barkley's little grandson, who could not pronounce the words vice president. The nearest he could come was "Veep," so Barkley became The Veep to one and all.

Barkley's humor rescued the Senate from many a dull moment. Once, when a Tennessee senator complained that another senator had yawned during his speech, Barkley proclaimed, "The yawn of the Senator from Illinois will be stricken from the record."

Barkley also turned up at practically every blossom festival on the block as President Truman's representative and an enthusiastic practitioner of what Barkley called "the osculatory business" of kissing beauty queens.

In 1952, when Truman announced his plans to retire, Barkley tried for the presidential nomination, but he was seventy-four years old and his eyes were failing, so he dropped out of the running. One might think he'd have been content with forty years of public service, but he wasn't.

He returned to the Senate in 1954. Two years later, he was giving a talk at Washington and Lee University. During a pause for applause, he dropped dead.

---

171. It can be seen today in a glass case in the Rotunda of the Capitol.
172. Since that comes to almost 3600 miles a day, one must conclude he simply shouted his speeches from the airplane as it flew by.

· 36 ·

Just What the
Committee Ordered

RICHARD M. NIXON
vice president under Dwight D. Eisenhower,
1953–1961

The summer of 1948 was a slow one in Washington, D.C., and the House
Committee on Un-American Activities was hard pressed to preserve its
reputation as a busy body. To pass the time, it was looking into a series
of events that had taken place eighteen years previously.

The committee had rounded up a witness named Whittaker Chambers and was taking his word for everything. Chambers was, after all, an
editor of *Time* magazine and admitted he'd belonged to a Communist
cell[173] in Washington during the thirties, so why should he lie about
anything else?

---

173. Communists had cells in those days. Today they live on plots.

Chambers kept insisting that another member of the cell was a man named Alger Hiss, who besides having a villainous-sounding name had served a term in the State Department during the intervening years. Called to account, Hiss denied knowing Chambers or sitting in his cell.

Well, it was hot, and most of the folks on the committee wanted to go fishing. But not Richard Milhous Nixon. Nixon, nearing the end of his freshman term in Congress, had been classified in a newspaper's appraisal of freshmen congressmen as "the greenest in town,"[174] so he had to do something: he was up for reelection that fall.

Plugging away at Alger Hiss, Nixon preyed on his birdwatcher's pride and got Hiss to admit that he had seen a rare prothonotary warbler in a swampy area by the Potomac, just as Whittaker Chambers had claimed.[175] Chambers also produced a set of documents called the Pumpkin Papers,[176] which proved to have been typed on Alger Hiss's typewriter. The rest is modern history: Hiss went to jail, and Richard Milhous Nixon went on to become vice president of the United States.

Nixon's early career was not especially promising. Upon graduating from Duke University law school, he sent job applications to a New York law firm and the Federal Bureau of Investigation. Both turned him down. His hopes dashed, he returned to his home town of

---

174. His tenderness toward colored people dates back to that stinging slur.
175. It still doesn't sound quite kosher. Most people, asked to describe a friend, don't ever think to say, "Well, there was that time he saw a rare prothonotary warbler in a swampy area by the Potomac."
176. Pumpkin was the name of the man who xeroxed them and gave them to the *Times*.

Whittier, California, to practice law just in case he ever got a chance to use it again.

Somewhere along in here Nixon married Thelma Catherine Patricia Ryan, who, asked if a poor girl from a little mining town in Nevada could find happiness with one of the nation's least-known lawyers, answered yes.

During World War II, Nixon joined the Navy and went off to the South Pacific, where he did something and became a lieutenant commander. He was hanging around Baltimore waiting for his discharge in 1946 when a friend called him from California and asked him if he was a Republican. It seems this committee of one hundred desperate California Republicans had chipped in to advertise for a young man with no previous political experience to run for Congress. Nixon was just what the committee ordered. With its approval and backing, Nixon ran and won.

The first lesson he learned was that—in California, anyway—the first candidate to call his opponent a liberal wins. By 1948, though, he hardly had to call anybody anything. He had received so much favorable publicity for flushing Alger Hiss out of that swampy area by the Potomac, he was a shoo-in. By 1950 he was ready for the big time.

Trampling light-heartedly over his opponent, Helen Gahagan Douglas, Nixon arrived in the Senate, where his crusading spirit caught the attention and admiration of General Dwight D. Eisenhower. Eisenhower's political background was remarkably similar to Nixon's: a committee of desperate Republicans had chipped in to advertise for an old man with no previous political experience to run for president, and they had asked Eisenhower if he was a Republican. Eisenhower decided he was—it wasn't easy, because a committee of desperate Democrats had just asked him the same thing—and threw his hat in the ring. And that was how it came to pass that Richard Nixon was picked for the vice presidential slot in 1952.

Nixon almost didn't get to be vice president. Two months after his nomination, a dirty liberal newspaper in New York ran a story about a Secret Nixon Fund to which a dedicated band of California Republicans regularly contributed. There was only one thing to do. Nixon decided to go on television and bare his soul to the American People.

This he did so effectively that by the end of what came to be called Nixon's "Checkers Speech" there wasn't a dry eye in the nation. Most of the tears shed were for Pat Nixon, who, as her husband lamented, "doesn't have a mink coat." But a few were shed for Nixon himself after he confessed that he had indeed taken a gift. "It was a little cocker spaniel dog," he began. "Black and white, spotted, and our little girl Tricia named it Checkers."[177] Once over the most emotional part, Nixon made one thing perfectly clear: "that regardless of what they say about it, we are going to keep it."

Well, the next day everybody was ecstatic about the show, and Nixon got to keep both the vice presidential nomination and the cocker spaniel

---

177. After her father's political career.

We don't know what Nixon was bragging about. Here's a typical American kitchen, and the only way in which it might be considered slightly superior to a Russian kitchen is that it has more ears of corn on the floor.

dog, black and white, spotted. Eisenhower met with Nixon and said, "You're my boy!" in front of everybody. And to top things off, Eisenhower read reporters a letter of recommendation he'd received from Nixon's mother. That clinched it.

Nixon's vice presidential career was one of almost feverish activity. Ike had commanded that all doors, cabinets, and file drawers be opened to the vice president, and he never forgot to invite Nixon to meetings. Nixon even subbed for the President at cabinet meetings when Eisenhower was hung up looking for his ball in the rough off the dogleg on the fifteenth hole. Eisenhower also had health reasons for not showing up. During the course of his eight years in the presidency, he suffered from a heart attack, ileitis, and a stroke, in that order. But he always got better, so Nixon never had to take over the government.

During Nixon's eight years as vice president, he traveled to fifty-four countries, mostly on goodwill tours. In July, 1959, he went to Moscow to open an American National Exhibition there. Khrushchev turned up for the opening, and he and Nixon got into a terrible argument about which country had slicker kitchens. The bragging match went on to washing machines and rockets, and Nixon shook his fist in Krushchev's face. Everybody was very impressed.

On another goodwill trip, this time to Latin America, the Nixons incited more spit than anything else. When they arrived in Venezuela, there were so many Communits spitting on them as they stood listening to the band play an anthem, they thought it was raining. And on the way into Caracas, the spit was so dense the Nixon's chauffeur had to turn on the windshield wipers. Ugh!

By 1960, with Ike retiring to the farm, Nixon decided he was ready for the presidency, but the nation thought otherwise and elected John F.

Kennedy instead. A lesser man might have given up, but Nixon just went back to California to plan ahead. Two years after his presidential defeat he ran for governor of California and lost. This time he realized he just wasn't leadership timber, and he dropped out of politics for good and for all.

· 37 ·

All the Way with LBJ

LYNDON B. JOHNSON
vice president under John F. Kennedy,
1961–November 22, 1963

If Lyndon Baines Johnson hadn't had such a good job already, he might have been elected president instead of vice president in 1960. As majority leader of the Senate, poor old Lyndon was stuck in the capital while Kennedy and Humphrey, who were just plain senators, roamed the land kissing babies and giving speeches.

By the time the Senate finally adjourned, Johnson had only five days before the convention to catch up. So the best he could do at the convention was the number two spot—the vice presidency.

Nobody, including the Kennedys, really thought he would take it. He didn't need the vice presidency as a stepping-stone, like Nixon; and he wasn't an old man, like Garner. Friends like Sam Rayburn helped talk Johnson into accepting the nomination in the interests of party unity.

It was also in the interests of selling the Democratic ticket in the South, where there was a widespread belief that if John F. Kennedy got to be president, the pope would be secretary of state.[178] Johnson's assignment was a toughie, but in Dallas he got an unexpected assist from a surly group of right-wing hecklers.

As Johnson and his wife, Claudia Alta Taylor Johnson, known to her friends as Lady Bird, entered a Dallas hotel, a bunch of Birchers, shouting insults, jostled the Johnsons and spat in their direction.[179] It was a bad mistake. The eyes of Texas were upon them, via television, and if there's anything that gets a Texan's dander up it's the sight of a person spitting at a lady. Kennedy won the election by a margin of 34 electoral votes, 24 of which were from Texas.[180]

Kennedy was so grateful to Johnson, he gave him all kinds of important things to do. Besides sitting in on cabinet meetings and National Security Council meetings, Johnson was made chairman of the Aeronautics and Space Council and also of the Peace Corps National Advisory Council. He was also asked to make sure the government minded its own advice on civil rights. He traveled like mad.

Johnson was a man who had raised the simple social custom of shaking hands almost to an occult art. In twenty-seven years, he had, as one writer notes, "twisted more wings yet ruffled fewer feathers than any other politician around." Now the world had a chance to witness the

---

178. A year or two later, everybody was wishing Kennedy *had* selected the pope.
179. What is all this spitting? We never had that when *we* were children.
180. A classic demonstration of what happens when you spit into the wind.

magic spectacle of Lyndon B. Johnson "pressing the flesh," as he called the ceremony of shaking hands.

All over the globe went he—to Senegal, Vietnam, Hong Kong, Formosa, India, Pakistan, and other outposts of the American Empire—slapping villagers on the back and saying howdy to everyone in sight. Ambassadors fainted dead away when they heard he was coming. They thought he was just too folksy for words. But the crowds loved him, and as Lyndon himself retorted, "What dignity are we trying to prove—that of the office of vice president or that of the human race?"

Occasionally, though, Johnson outdid himself in the dignity of the human race department. One day he arrived home from work and told Lady Bird he had a surprise for her. Its name was Bashir Ahmed. Bashir Ahmed was this Pakistani camel driver who'd been minding his own business, waiting to cross the road with a load of sacked straw, when Johnson passed him on the way into Karachi from the airport. "Come and see me sometime," said Johnson, pressing Bashir's flesh. To the Vice President's great surprise, when he got back to the States he received word that the camel driver had decided to accept the invitation. It could have been a disaster, but the Johnsons' Southern hospitality and the camel driver's poetic soul melded beautifully, and the visit was a smash hit in terms of public relations with Pakistan. Johnson did a lot of other good things as vice president. He went to Rome for a chat with Pope John, and he flew to Berlin when The Wall went up to assure the people there that we wouldn't desert them. He was also very careful about clearing everything with the White House, so he never got in trouble with the boss.

There wasn't even a personality conflict, though Kennedy and Johnson were two different breeds of cat. Johnson was just a generation removed from log cabin days. His grandmother had once hidden from

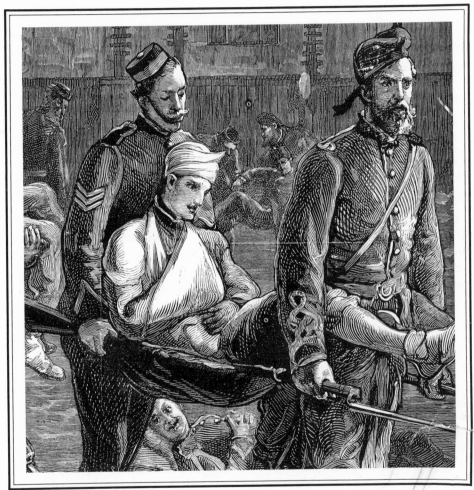

The French ambassador being helped to a cab by two White House aides after shaking hands with Lyndon Johnson at a diplomatic reception.

Indian attackers in a flour barrel. Kennedy's family had buckets of money which they'd acquired in Boston, where it was easy to pick up class if you had the money to support the habit. No Kennedy had ever hidden in a flour barrel for any reason.

Nobody ever accused Johnson of having too much class. He was Just Folks all the way. And his folksiness increased, rather than diminished, when he got to be president after Kennedy's assassination.

For one thing, the nation got to see more of him when he displayed the scar from his gall bladder operation over network television. He also lost the beagle vote by picking his pet beagles up by their long ears in front of reporters.

At the close of the 1960 election campaign, Lady Bird had announced that she and her husband were "going back to the ranch tomorrow and be just plain vegetables for a few days." With the approach of the 1968 elections, Johnson declined to run again, which pleased Lady Bird no end for it meant they could be just plain vegetables for the rest of their days.

· 38 ·

The Drugstore Liberal

HUBERT H. HUMPHREY
vice president under Lyndon B. Johnson, 1965–1969

Hubert Horatio Humphrey is the only vice president of the United States ever married to a lady named Muriel.[181] On top of that, he comes from Minnesota.

Humphrey started out as a pharmacist, which is why he is sometimes called a Drugstore Liberal.[182] He was born poor, and he lost what little money he'd managed to accumulate by running against John F.

---

181. He was also the only vice president whose three initials were the same. Oh, there was William Wheeler, but he had a middle name beginning with A. Charles Curtis didn't have a middle name, and Calvin Coolidge's middle name was Calvin (he didn't use his first name, John). People like Levi P. Morton and Charles W. Fairbanks didn't even come close.
182. To distinguish him from Jewelry Shop Liberals, Podiatrist Liberals, and Pawnbroker Liberals.

Kennedy in the primary elections of 1960. Politically speaking, he was something of a boy wonder. He'd been mayor of Minneapolis at 34 and a United States senator three years later. As soon as he got to the Senate he started flailing around, tilting at greybeards and generally making trouble for everybody.

One of the things he kept flailing and tilting about was civil rights. He was for them. And at the national convention of 1948, Humphrey insisted that the convention adopt a stronger plank on civil rights than the one provided by the administration. Some people approved of Humphrey's plank, but many others tried to jump up and down on it until it splintered.

The diehard element was so disenchanted with him, it disassociated itself from the convention and the party, forming a separate group called the Dixiecrats because most of its members came from Dixie. One of the group was Strom Thurmond,[183] who didn't think becoming a Dixiecrat took it far enough. He later became a Republican.

Humphrey was described by the Kennedy forces as a "good speaker," which is putting it mildly. Humphrey is one of the great long-distance speakers of modern times, and if this country ever has to meet Castro in a debating match, Humphrey's our man. Long years of practice on the Senate floor have enabled the ebullient senator from Minnesota to speak for two or three hours on any given subject and maybe two or three more on subjects which have *not* been given.

When Lyndon Johnson became Kennedy's vice president, he said he

---

183. Don't apologize. He was used to people erroneously calling him Storm.

As soon as Hubert Humphrey got to the Senate, he started flailing around.

wanted to be "the kind of vice president I would want if I were president." Now he had the chance to pick his own running mate, and the choice fell on Hubert Horatio Humphrey. Had Lyndon B. Johnson been trying to be like Humphrey all those months?

In 1964 Robert F. Kennedy was a lot of people's favorite candidate for the vice presidency. But he wasn't Lyndon B. Johnson's, and that's what counted. In order to eliminate Kennedy from the running without hurting his feelings, Johnson felt compelled to rule out the entire cabinet, of which Kennedy was a member. Thus the only person left to be vice president was Hubert H. Humphrey.

Humphrey was absolutely delighted by the prospect. He'd tried to become vice president once before, when Adlai Stevenson was running for the presidency in 1956, but he'd lost to Estes Kefauver, whose name was judged to be more mellifluous than Hubert Horatio Humphrey's. He'd also lost the primaries and his modest fortune by running against John Kennedy in 1960. But he kept on hoping, and now his hopes were coming true.

The President summoned Humphrey to Washington to tell him the good news. When Humphrey got to Washington, he found a messenger sent to him to tell him to lie low for a while so that his arrival wouldn't upstage Lady Bird's big entrance at the convention in Atlantic City. So Humphrey drove around in a taxi for three hours, and by the time he got to the White House he had fallen asleep.

Johnson made Humphrey promise he would be a good vice president and not disagree with the President. This done, the President departed for Atlantic City, where he broke all the rules by giving a speech for Humphrey even before Humphrey's name had been put into the hat. It was the sort of thing only a president could get away with.

Humphrey was such a good vice president, Johnson decided the kid should have a term of his own when he and Lady Bird retired to Texas to become vegetables. It seemed like an easy thing to arrange. After all, the 1968 convention was being held in Chicago, which, as luck would have it, had acquired another Democratic mayor. Hubert Horatio Humphrey did win the nomination for the presidency, largely because he and his friends were about the only people allowed into the hall. But that's as far as he got.

· 39 ·

Spiro Who?

SPIRO T. AGNEW
vice president under Richard M. Nixon, 1969–

Spiro Agnew is a household word.[184]

184. Here are some others: Adolph's Meat Tenderizer, Elmer's Glue, Schlitz Beer, Sunsweet Prune Juice, Pantene Hair Spray, Carnation Milk, Alcoa Wrap, Midol, Johnny Walker Red Label Scotch, Sony Television, Gallo Wine, Singer Sewing Machines, One-A-Day Vitamins, Ford Motor Cars, Wesson Oil, Tabu Perfume, Pall Mall Cigarettes, Log Cabin Syrup, Chicken of the Sea Tuna, Heinz Baked Beans, Campbell's Soups, Saran Wrap, Sherwin-Williams Paint, Bold Detergent, Feminique Deodorant Spray, Coca-Cola, Supp-Hose, Sealy Posturepedic Mattress, *Better Homes & Gardens,* Del Monte Vegetables, Dairylea Milk, Pepperidge Farm Breads, Sanka, Kraft Cheese, Sara Lee Cakes, Camay Soap, Breck Shampoo, Bird's Eye Frozen Foods, Kleenex Tissues, Kent Cigarettes, Haig & Haig Blended Whiskey, Schick Electric Shaver, *Time* Magazine, Kodak Instamatic Camera, Knox Gelatin, Toyota Automobiles, *TV Guide,* Heineken's Beer, English Leather

The average American household consumes 10.5 lbs. of lard per year.

Cologne, Jantzen Bathing Suits, Clairol Shampoo, Holland House Mix, Crest Toothpaste, Whirlpool Washer, *McCall's,* Big John's Beans 'n Fixin's, Ronrico Rum, Norelco Electric Shaver, Reynolds Wrap, Mystic Tape, Pepsi-Cola, Zenith Television, Right Guard Deodorant Spray, Max Factor Cosmetics, Charmin Toilet Tissue, Bumblebee Tuna, Bali Undergarments, Smirnoff Vodka, Tame Hair Rinse, Savarin Coffee, Bond Bread, Polaroid Swinger, Oldsmobile, Smucker's Preserves, Skippy Peanut Butter, Plymouth, Realemon, Hellman's Mayonnaise, Old Granddad Bourbon, Charles of the Ritz Cosmetics, Miller's Beer, General Electric Dryer, Kool Cigarettes, H-O Cream Farina, Domino Sugar, Dodge, Kellog's Corn Flakes, *Atlantic* Magazine, Marlboro Cigarettes, Diamond Matches, Betty Crocker Cake Mix, Gold Medal Flour, Bombay Gin, Chun King Soy Sauce, Nabisco Crackers, Goodman's Noodles, Helena Rubinstein Cosmetics, Benson & Hedges Cigarettes, Sylvania Radios, Canada Dry Soda, French's Mustard, Hershey's Chocolates, Kayser Hosiery, Frigidaire Refrigerators, White Owl Cigars, Colgate Toothpaste, etc., etc., etc.